The Doge's Palace in Venice

The Doge's Palace in Venice

Electa

MUSEI
CIVICI
VENEZIANI

MUSEI CIVICI VENEZIANI

Texts
Giandomenico Romanelli
Monica da Cortà Fumei
Enrico Basaglia

Coordination
Monica da Cortà Fumei

Translation
Jeremy Scott

Editorial Coordination
Cristina Garbagna

Editing
Paola Bertelli

Graphic Coordination
Dario Tagliabue

Page Layout
Lucia Vigo

Technical Coordination
Andrea Panozzo

Quality Control
Giancarlo Berti

Cover
Vittore Carpaccio,
The Lion of St. Mark, *1516.*
Venice, Doge's Palace,
Sala Grimani.

Page 2
Lazzaro Bastiani, Portrait
of Francesco Foscari, *1460.*
Venice, Museo Correr.

Reprint 2005
First Edition 2004

© Musei Civici Veneziani

An editorial realization by Mondadori Electa S.p.A., Milan

www.museiciviciveneziani.it
www.electaweb.it

Contents

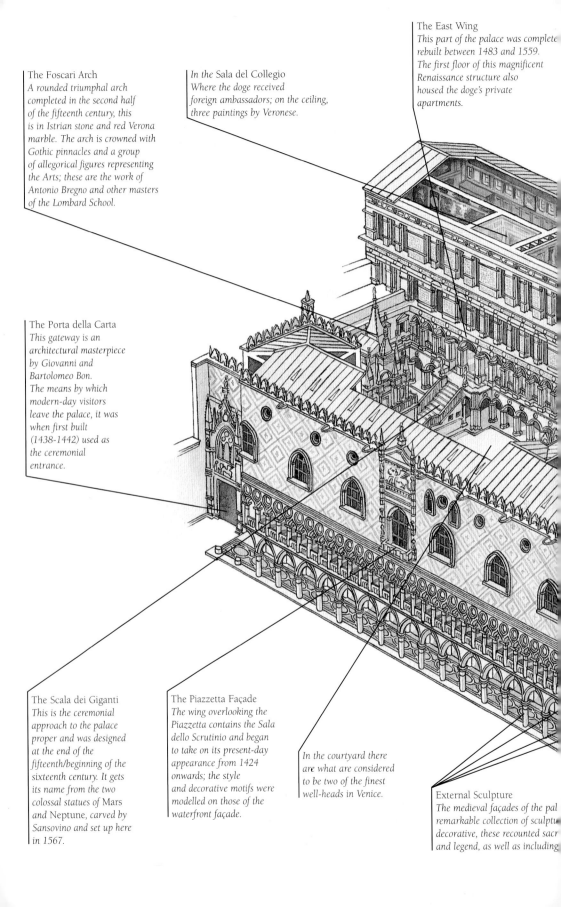

The East Wing
This part of the palace was complete
rebuilt between 1483 and 1559.
The first floor of this magnificent
Renaissance structure also
housed the doge's private
apartments.

In the Sala del Collegio
Where the doge received
foreign ambassadors; on the ceiling,
three paintings by Veronese.

The Foscari Arch
A rounded triumphal arch
completed in the second half
of the fifteenth century, this
is in Istrian stone and red Verona
marble. The arch is crowned with
Gothic pinnacles and a group
of allegorical figures representing
the Arts; these are the work of
Antonio Bregno and other masters
of the Lombard School.

The Porta della Carta
This gateway is an
architectural masterpiece
by Giovanni and
Bartolomeo Bon.
The means by which
modern-day visitors
leave the palace, it was
when first built
(1438-1442) used as
the ceremonial
entrance.

The Scala dei Giganti
This is the ceremonial
approach to the palace
proper and was designed
at the end of the
fifteenth/beginning of the
sixteenth century. It gets
its name from the two
colossal statues of Mars
and Neptune, carved by
Sansovino and set up here
in 1567.

The Piazzetta Façade
The wing overlooking the
Piazzetta contains the Sala
dello Scrutinio and began
to take on its present-day
appearance from 1424
onwards; the style
and decorative motifs were
modelled on those of the
waterfront façade.

**In the courtyard there
are what are considered
to be two of the finest
well-heads in Venice.**

External Sculpture
The medieval façades of the pal
remarkable collection of sculptu
decorative, these recounted sacr
and legend, as well as including

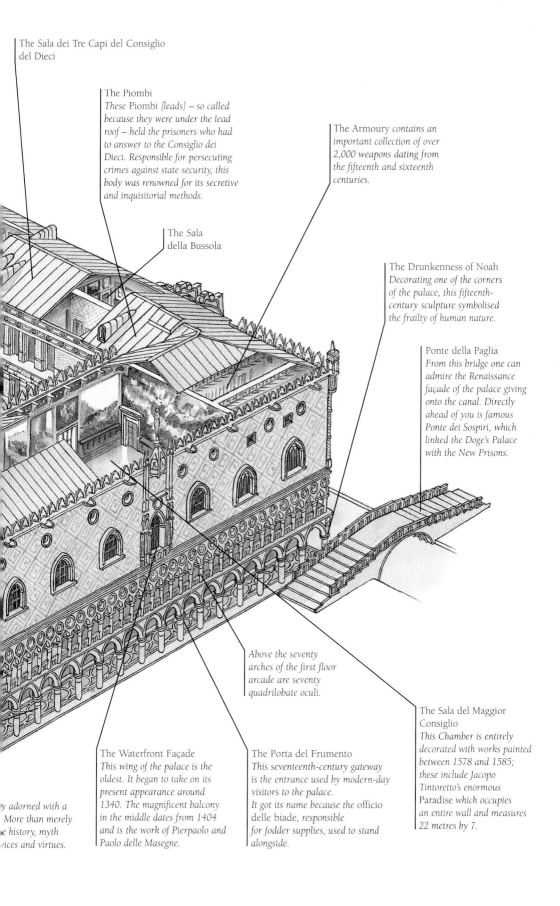

The Sala dei Tre Capi del Consiglio del Dieci

The Piombi
These Piombi [leads] – so called because they were under the lead roof – held the prisoners who had to answer to the Consiglio dei Dieci. Responsible for persecuting crimes against state security, this body was renowned for its secretive and inquisitorial methods.

The Armoury *contains an important collection of over 2,000 weapons dating from the fifteenth and sixteenth centuries.*

The Sala della Bussola

The Drunkenness of Noah
Decorating one of the corners of the palace, this fifteenth-century sculpture symbolised the frailty of human nature.

Ponte della Paglia
From this bridge one can admire the Renaissance façade of the palace giving onto the canal. Directly ahead of you is famous Ponte dei Sospiri, which linked the Doge's Palace with the New Prisons.

Above the seventy arches of the first floor arcade are seventy quadrilobate oculi.

The Sala del Maggior Consiglio
This Chamber is entirely decorated with works painted between 1578 and 1585; these include Jacopo Tintoretto's enormous Paradise which occupies an entire wall and measures 22 metres by 7.

The Waterfront Façade
This wing of the palace is the oldest. It began to take on its present appearance around 1340. The magnificent balcony in the middle dates from 1404 and is the work of Pierpaolo and Paolo delle Masegne.

The Porta del Frumento
This seventeenth-century gateway is the entrance used by modern-day visitors to the palace. It got its name because the officio delle biade, responsible for fodder supplies, used to stand alongside.

y adorned with a More than merely e history, myth ices and virtues.

The City and the Palace

The creation of the Doge's Palace in effect marks the birth of Venice as a city. In 810, having finally repelled the forces of King Pepin, son of Charlemagne and Lord of Italy, Doge Agnello Partecipazio decided to move the *palatium ducis* from Malamocco – judged too open to assault from the sea – to the more central, and easily defended, islands of Rialto. A few years later – in 828 – the adventurous escapades of Bono da Malamocco and Rustico da Torcello resulted in the body of the evangelist St. Mark being brought from Alexandria in Egypt to Rialto. Thereafter, Venice had its essential core structure (a walled ducal castle) and a revered foundation myth, regarding a saint whose final resting-place in the lagoon was said to be the fulfilment of a prophecy. This was enough to attract the Veneto-Latin settlers who two centuries earlier had fled from the Longobard invasion of the mainland to such places as Eraclea, Cittanova, Torcello, Olivolo and Malamocco – communities which after the fall of Ravenna in 751 had remained the last Byzantine outposts in Western Europe. The new city expanded and grew in strength; and its liege status with regard to Byzantium

The Transport of the Body of St. Mark, tenth-fourteenth century. Detail of the Pala d'Oro. Venice, St. Mark's Basilica.

The Transport of the Body of St. Mark into the Basilica, tenth-fourteenth century. Detail of the Pala d'Oro. Venice, St. Mark's Basilica.

gradually became little more than a pretext for maintaining its privileged position in trade with the East, the very basis of Venice's fortunes. Venetian naval power was, in fact, the only force that could withstand Saracen and Slav raids within the Adriatic, and thus the new city began to enjoy further commercial privileges – for example, in its trade relations with the German empire to the north. However, the Venetian system of government had yet to be established.

The palace was still first and foremost the fortified residence of a doge against whose personal ambitions the community as a whole had no other resort than violence: in 976, for example, there was an armed revolt that resulted in the destruction of the palace, the basilica, a good part of the surrounding buildings, and the dynastic aspirations of the Candiano family, which had provided five doges over the previous century (engaging in skulduggery and plotting that had risked compromising the delicate political equilibrium of the Venetian economy). Rapidly rebuilt, the new palace was ready to receive Doge Pietro Orseolo on his return from the triumphant naval expedition that had made Venice master of Istria and Dalmatia. And the following year the building's oriental magnificence would make a strong impression upon the Holy Roman Emperor Otto III. His secret visit to the city was intended to gain Venice's support in his struggle against the feudal lords of Italy, but it proved largely unsuccessful: now a power in its own right, the city had learnt how to play that difficult diplomatic game of remaining equidistant from all the great powers of Europe and the Mediterranean in order to profit from the differences between them. In 1082 the victory of the Venetian fleet over the Normans of Sicily would lead to the Byzantine emperor granting the city such a privileged position in the Eastern Mediterranean that thirteen years later Venice could afford to look on with bemused detachment as preparations for the First Crusade got underway; this detachment,

Domenico Robusti, known as Tintoretto, Portraits of Doge Pietro IV Candiano and Pietro I Orseolo, 1580-1590. Venice, Doge's Palace, Sala del Maggior Consiglio.

Francesco Grisellini and Giustino Menescardi, Italy, Greece and Asia Minor, 1762. Venice, Doge's Palace, Sala dello Scudo.

however, did not prevent the city from making sure that it – rather than Genoa or Pisa – gained control of the best markets in the newly-founded Christian kingdoms of Syria and the Holy Land that would result from the conquest of Jerusalem. Clearly, the range of Venetian interests had now become too complex to be governed by a doge elected simply by an ill-defined "popular assembly." In a republic where every political decision might effect profits and losses, the organs of government had to be answerable to the people who were, in effect, the shareholders in "Venice Inc." – that is, those whose wealth depended upon trade and commerce. The result of this need was the foundation of the Maggior Consiglio [Great Council], a sort of "shareholders' assembly" to which the doge, the Minor Consiglio [Minor Council] and all the other executive bodies that would be created over the centuries had to answer for every single decision made. The first in a long series of remarkable "chairmen" for Venice Inc. was the Doge Sebastiano Ziani, in 1172 began work on the entire re-organisation of St. Mark's Square area: the outside walls of the castle were demolished; the space reserved for the doge's residence was reduced in size; the entire wing of the palace giving onto the Piazzetta was destined to house the city's law-courts; and within the wing giving onto the waterfront work began on the first great council chamber for the Maggior Consiglio. By 1177 everything was ready to provide a worthy setting for an international triumph of Venetian diplomacy: the reconciliation which Doge Ziani had negotiated between Pope Alexander III and Emperor Frederick Barbarossa, who had been divided by the so-called "Investiture Contest." Then in 1204 would come the opportunity that raised Venice to the very acme of its power. Twelve years earlier Saladin had retaken Jerusalem, and the pope – together with numerous rulers in Europe – had proclaimed a Fourth Crusade. Forces from all over the continent converged upon Venice to take ship; but ships cost money, and these crusaders and soldiers-of-fortune did not have any. The solution to the problem was suggested by the old doge of the day, Enrico Dandolo: Venice would provide transport in exchange for help in re-taking the city of Zara, which had rebelled against Venetian sovereignty. That city fell without much trouble, and the doge began to see that this was a golden opportunity to settle accounts between Venice and the Byzantine empire once and for all. Upon the pretext of a palace revolt, the crusader forces forget the "Infidels" in the Holy Land and turned their arms instead against Constantinople. Its conquest brought with it what remained of the Roman empire in the East, and Doge Dandolo was rewarded with the ancient title of "lord of a half and of a quarter of the Empire of the Romans." For its part, Venice obtained an empire – in Greece, in the islands of the Mediterranean and in Anatolia – as well as the lion's share of the booty obtained from the despoliation of one of the richest cities in the history of the world. At his coronation in 1192 that same Enrico Dandolo had sworn an "undertaking" [*promissione*] that drastically limited the personal power of the doge. Venice became unchallenged master of the Eastern Mediterranean and its very lucrative trade. Obviously, the city's long-time rival, Genoa, could hardly stand back and watch this happen: plots were hatched with the Byzantines to undermine the new Latin empire, and with the "Infidels" to create trouble for Venetian bases wherever they were found.

Thus began almost two centuries of naval battles and pirate raids, of treacherous aggression and openly-negotiated alliances. In effect, this was a battle to the death between the two great maritime republics

Benedetto and Carlo Caliari, Pope Alexander III and Doge Sebastiano Ziani send Ambassadors to Emperor Frederick Barbarossa to Negotiate Peace, 1588-1590. Venice, Doge's Palace, Sala del Maggior Consiglio.

The Rainbow: the Pledge
of Divine Mercy, *first half
of the thirteenth century.
Venice, St. Mark's Basilica
(south vault).*

of Italy, for both of whom trade with the East was essential. As often
happens in contests where no holds are barred, the end came from
exhaustion: in 1380 Genoa occupied Chioggia, just to the south
of Venice, but would then be forced into unconditional surrender. The
negotiated end to hostilities came the following year, in the Peace
of Turin, with neither party emerging as a clear victor. However, over
the long term the effects for the two cities would be very different.
The great banking families of Genoa – the Doria, the Spinola and the
Fieschi – would continue to prosper for centuries, providing finance
for kings and emperors and leading their fleets into battle; but each
of them was essentially looking out for their own interests. After the
War of Chioggia, the Republic of Genoa went into rapid decline and
would ultimately lose its independence; from being a battle standard,

Column from the church of St. John at Acre, sixth century. Venice, St. Mark's Basilica (exterior).

the Genoese Cross of St. George would become the logo of a bank that gradually devoured the State. In Venice the long emergency would have the opposite effect: cohesion within the social body of the city was reinforced and the ruling classes made a series of institutional changes that resulted in the system of government that Venice would enjoy substantially unchanged until the fall of the Republic. Raised as a battle standard for the first time in 1257 – when Venetian ships defeated the Genoese fleet at St. John of Acre – the flag with the Lion of St. Mark would not be lowered until 1797. Given the increasing complexity of affairs, the Maggior Consiglio decided that it was too numerous to debate matters with sufficient expedition, and so in 1255 the Consiglio dei Pregadi – or the Senate – was set up; this was responsible for the management of city finances, trade and matters relating to the fleet. Over time, its duties – and the number of its members – would increase, until ultimately this became the main organ for all matters relating to the State. A veritable revolution in the city's institutional framework took place in 1297, when the number of members of the Maggior Consiglio was increased from 400 (elected by representatives of the six sestieri – districts – of Venice) to 1,200 permanent members (all those who had been part of the Maggior Consiglio during the previous three years). Drawn from around 200 different families, these 1,200 then obtained a ruling that a seat on the

Council was hereditary – and thus the Venetian patrician class defined itself appropriating exclusive exercise of political rights and duties. Revolutions are never painless, and the years that followed were very turbulent. In 1310 an attempted coup headed by the Tiepolo and Querini families would lead to a pitched battle and in 1335 the doge himself – Marino Faliero – would be beheaded for "treason." State security was at this point entrusted to a special committee which subsequently became a permanent body – the so-called Consiglio dei Dieci [Council of Ten]. The palace as built by Doge Ziani had not

Venice, St. Mark's Basilica, north façade.

envisaged these changes; and between 1340 and 1368, after the social unrest had come to an end, work was carried out on the waterfront side of the building to create an enormous new chamber that would provide a fitting setting for the enlarged Maggior Consiglio. This was the first side of the palace to take on its present-day appearance.

But whilst Venice's internal political structure was being defined, the international situation remained remarkably fluid. In the East, the anaemic remnants of the Eastern Empire and the Arab potentates of Egypt and Palestine were all gradually losing ground before the irresistible westward advance of an enemy that was as yet an unknown quantity: the Turkish warriors from the Asian steppes who in 1453 would conquer Constantinople itself. All the sources of Venice's wealth – in Egypt, the Black Sea and Greece – gradually fell into the hands of an adversary whose one goal would, for centuries to come, be the constant expansion of his own already-enormous power. From this point onwards, operations in the Eastern Mediterranean could no longer rely on blandishments and the occasional threat to obtain commercial privileges and monopolies; now it was a question of fighting, desperately, in order to keep hold of what the city already possessed. And in Italy, too, things had changed, The city communes of the Po Valley were now in the hands of aggressive lords – the Carraresi, the Scaligeri, the Visconti, etc. – who were warriors rather than merchants, and more than willing to use war to extend their own territories at the expense of their neighbours. The risk was that, in holding aloof from this nest of vipers, Venice would find its trade routes to the rich markets of the north interrupted or, even worse, have at its back an army powerful enough to invade the lagoon. The choice to be made was the subject of extensive debate, with the (numerous) conservatives arguing that Venice was a sea-power only; however, the innovators, the so-called "partito della Terraferma" [terra firma party] would eventually win the day. Funds and equipment were set aside for mainland campaigns; mercenaries and *condottieri* were hired; the city negotiated alliances which it knew were to be very temporary indeed; and the attack began. Treviso had already become a Venetian bridgehead by 1339; in 1404-1405 the Republic took Padua, which had long been a thorn in its side, Vicenza and Verona; in 1418-1423, Friuli and Istria fell; in 1431, it was the turn of the Lombard cities of Brescia, Bergamo and Cremona; and finally, in 1484, the mainland empire established its southern borders on the Po. By the end of the fifteenth century, the "Stato di Terraferma" made the Venetian Republic the largest territorial power in Italy. This had been the century of Francesco Foscari, an indefatigable promoter of territorial expansion, whose election as doge in 1423 marked the victory of the so-called "innovators." But Foscari would pay dearly for his determination: after thirty years of triumphs and victories, he would, in 1457, become the only doge ever forced to abdicate. Nevertheless, he did leave an indelible mark on the new wing of the palace, commissioning various extant parts of the strucutre: the room that in 1468 would be used to house the Greek and Latin treasures which Cardinal Bessarione had saved from the Turkish; the Foscari loggia; the magnificent Porta della Carta surmounted by a statue of the doge himself; and the Foscari Porch that leads into the palace courtyard. Over the next fifty years, the wing destined to house the doge's private apartments would be raised; complete with imposing Renaissance façade, this would also contain an entire floor given over to council chambers for the various committees of government. As has been mentioned, Venice was by this point the largest territorial power in Italy; and its "arrogance" attracted the wrath of the warrior Pope Julius II, the French (who had established themselves in Milan) and the Habsburg emperor (who wanted "his" Friuli back). At Cambrai the European powers signed an anti-Venice alliance, and in a single day – at the battle of Agnadello (1509) – the Republic lost all its mainland possessions. A tenacious campaign led on the battlefield itself by Doge Andrea Gritti would, over the following decade, result in the recovery of these possessions;

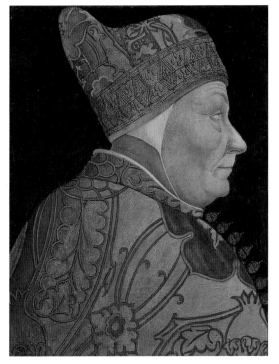

Lazzaro Bastiani, Portrait of Francesco Foscari, *1460. Venice, Museo Correr.*

Vittore Carpaccio, The Lion of St. Mark, *1516. Venice, Doge's Palace, Sala Grimani.*

however, Venice had learnt a bitter lesson.which made it more receptive to the prudent advice of the "conservatives." Power politics within Europe was now the preserve of such giants as France, Spain and the Holy Roman Empire, which could all draw on the resources of huge territories. With the discovery of America and of new routes to the East, most trade traffic was now moving outside the Mediterranean to the Atlantic; it was the countries that bordered on that ocean which now became the dominant powers. At this point, Venice fortified its existing position and fell back on the every more difficulty tactic of associating itself with neither one side nor the other. The Golden Age was over. But though trade was not what it had been, the "Stato di Terraferma" and the (still sizeable) remnants of Venice's overseas possessions meant the Republic could enjoy the ripeness of age with full magnificence. In this period of wars of religion, the tolerant city became one of the liveliest cultural centres on the continent; and the coherent pursuance of a policy of neutrality meant that the Republic enjoyed the respect, if not the friendship, of the powers of Europe. Of course another reason for this respect was that the Venetian fleet was the first line of defence against renewed Turkish expansionism in the Mediterranean – a terrible threat that seemed to restore the cohesion of a Christendom. The struggle was, however, very one-sided

and all that Venice could do was try as long as possible to follow
a policy of containment. One after another, the islands of the Aegean
were taken; then Venice lost its fortified settlements in Greece, and
in 1571 Cyprus, the jewel in the Venetian crown, fell after heroic
resistance. It was only then – with the Sultan's fleets at the very mouth
of the Adriatic, and his armies streaming through the Balkans –
that the pope, Spain and the Holy Roman Empire would work
coherently to give Venice the magnificent naval victory of Lepanto,
after which the Republic enjoyed a few years' breathing-space. Work
on the Doge's palace had meanwhile continued, and the erection
on the Scala dei Giganti of the colossal statues of *Mars* and *Neptune*
made a further contribution to the architectural development of the
whole; the prisons were at this time also transferred onto the other side
of the canal. However, from this time onwards, attention was focused
on the adornment of the interiors: the damage caused by more or less
disastrous fires was repaired (the blaze of 1574 would result in Palladio
drawing up new designs for the Sala delle Quattro Porte, the Sala del
Collegio and the Senato); and artists such as Tintoretto and Veronese
were commissioned to produce the great cycles of paintings that were
intended to celebrate the glories of the past. By now the very structure
of the Palace was seen as an architectural expression of Venice itself, of

Andrea Vicentino, The Battle of Lepanto, *1595-1605. Venice, Doge's Palace, Sala dello Scrutinio.*

Jacopo Palma il Giovane, Crowned by Victory, Venice Receives its Subject Provinces, *1582-1584. Venice, Doge's Palace, Sala del Maggior Consiglio.*

that principle of the "Venetian Exception" which had made it possible for the Republic to resist the conformism of the Counter-Reformation. Nevertheless, encircled though it was by the Habsburg powers of Spain and Austria, the Republic would in the early decades of the seventeenth century successfully withstand all attempts to make it toe the line – ideological pressure which Venice saw as an usurpation of its own freedoms. The pen of such a brilliant polemicist as Paolo Sarpi would certainly prove to be as mighty as the sword in opposing the 1606 interdict placed on the city by Pope Paul V. Then, in 1613-1617, Venice came to the verge of an open clash with Austria because of the latter's encouragement of Oskok pirate raids in the Adriatic; and in 1618 the Cosiglio dei Dieci had to deal in its own inimitably brusque way with a coup d'état plotted by the Spaniards. But following the outbreak of the Thirty Years' War the Habsburgs had other things to think about whilst Venice managed to remain neutral in the blood-letting that weakened Spain, France and Germany at the same time as it opened the way for the new maritime powers of Holland and England to gain control of the oceans. The Republic would, however, be shaken when the sultan's fleet appeared off the port of Candy in Crete in 1645 – the first sign of a new phase in Turkish expansionism. Using all the resources at its command, Venice would fight to the last, holding onto this final bastion of its colonial empire until 1669. Finance for the war was raised by the sale of seats in the Maggior Consiglio. However, even this was not enough; the "Venetian system" was beginning to show its weaknesses, and was proving incapable of rejuvenating itself. The last warrior-hero of the Serenissima was Doge Francesco Morosini, "the Peloponnesian," who in 1669 snatched back the Peloponnese from the Turks, but just for a few years. Decline was by now irreversible. The city had become a sort of curiosity, a fantastic playground for the scions of the European nobility, an example offered by the new theorists of the Enlightenment of an archaic system of arbitrary aristocratic rule. For many, the Doge's Palace was nothing more than the seat of a "toothless" Maggior Consiglio which represented no-one but itself, which had sunk into being the preserve of a group of old schemers who were arrogant towards the weak, supine towards the powerful. A single shove would have brought the whole political edifice tumbling down; and Venice survived solely because of the Ancien Regime's respect for a political tradition. However, Napoleon had the whole world to conquer and no time to waste. Without a single shot being fired, in 1797 he obtained from the timid last Doge, Ludovico Manin, Venice's signature to its own death sentence. The city was then occupied and numerous of its art treasures shipped off to Paris; thereafter, Venice served merely as a pawn in international power politics, being ceded to Austria. There was a revolt against the French led by the common people (the nobility did not raise a finger). The old battle standard of the Lion of St. Mark would only be raised once more: during the revolutionary period of 1848-49, when the city resisted the Austrians and became the seat of a provisional Republican government headed by Daniele Manin. Thereafter, for an entire century, the Doge's Palace became home to the offices, law-courts and institutions of a foreign power. In 1924 it would become a museum.

Giandomenico Tiepolo,
The New World, *1791-1793 (detail). Venice, Ca' Rezzonico, Museum of Eighteenth-Century Venice.*

The History of the Doge's Palace

In 810 Doge Angelo Partecipazio moved the seat of government from the island of Malamocco to the area of Rivoalto (the present-day Rialto). It was at this period that it was decided to built a *palatium duci*, a ducal palace. The model chosen for this structure may have been the Palace of Diocletian at Spalato; however, no trace remains of that ninth-century building. Though we do not know with certainty what that old palace looked like, it is probable that it was an agglomeration of different buildings destined to serve various purposes, the whole thing being protected by a canal, stout walls and massive corner towers. Traces of those fortifications and corner towers have survived. Reached by a large fortified gateway that was more or less where the Porta della Carta now stands, the buildings within these walls will have housed public offices, courtrooms, prisons, the doge's apartments, stables, armouries and other necessary facilities. The outline of crenellated walls that appears in the earliest extant Map of Venice – that drawn up by Fra' Paolino – may be taken as giving us a summary account of what the palace looked like. In the tenth century the palace was partially destroyed

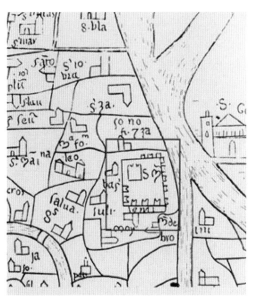

Fra' Paolino Minorita, Plan of Venice, 1346, detail of the St. Mark's area. Venice, Biblioteca Nazionale Marciana.

Venice, Fondaco dei Turchi.

by a fire, and the subsequent reconstruction work was undertaken at the behest of Doge Sebastiano Ziani (1172-1178, see p. 11). A great reformer, this doge would radically change the layout of the entire area of St. Mark's Square. For his palace, he had two new structures built: one giving onto the Piazzetta (to house courts and legal institutions) and the other overlooking St. Mark's Basin (to house government institutions). Thus the old castle which had been closed in upon itself was opened outwards, to meet the needs of a city that was developing and expanding in political, social and economic terms. What did these new palace structures look like? Probably, they had all the characteristic features of Byzantine-Venetian architecture, of which the Fondaco dei Turchi is a typical example. Only a few traces of this period of building works remain: parts of a ground-level wall base in Istrian stone and some herring-bone-pattern brick paving. At the end of the thirteenth century it became necessary to extend the palace once more. Political changes in 1297 – the so-called "Serrata del Maggior Consiglio" [Closure of the Great Council] – led to a considerable increase in the number of people who had the right to participate in the meetings of that legislative assembly (the "closure" had, in fact, led to the number of the Maggior Consiglio's members increasing from four hundred to one thousand two hundred). Hence, the need for a radical re-thinking of the palace, in the new language of Gothic architecture. The work, which would result in the building that is familiar to us today, started around 1340 under Doge Bartolomeo Gradenigo (1339-1343) and was concerned principally with the so-called Palazzo del Governo – that is, the side of the palace overlooking the lagoon. Documentary evidence enables us to identify some of the craftsmen involved in this stage of the work: for example, in 1361, a certain Filippo Calendario was appointed as stonemason/sculptor and a Pietro Basejo as *magister prothus* [foreman]. In 1365 the Paduan artist Guariento was commissioned to decorate the east wall of the Sala del Maggior Consiglio with a large fresco; whilst the windows in the room are the work of the Delle Masegne family. A few decades later (1408-1416) Gentile da Fabriano and Pisanello completed the fresco decoration of the room; but the Maggior Consiglio only met there for the first time in 1419. In 1424, when Francesco Foscari was doge (1423-1457, see p. 17), it was decided to extend the rebuilding work to the wing overlooking the Piazzetta, which served as the law-courts. The new wing was designed as a continuation of that giving onto the waterfront: a ground-floor arcade on the outside, with open first-floor loggias running along the façade and the internal courtyard side of the wing. At the same level as the Sala del Maggior Consiglio was another vast room, known first as the Library and then as the Sala dello Scrutinio. The large windows and the pinnacled parapet took up the same decorative motifs as had been used on the waterfront façade. This Piazzetta façade was then completed with the construction of the Porta della Carta (1438-1442), the work of Giovanni and

Pier Paolo and Paolo Dalle Masegne, the balcony of the waterfront façade, 1404. Venice, Doge's Palace.

The Doge's Palace seen from the Piazzetta.

The Renaissance wing of the Doge's Palace.

Bartolomeo Bon. Work on the other wings of the palace would not come until later. These would start with the construction of the Foscari Porch beyond the Porta della Carta, culminating in the Foscari Arch. This work dragged on for some years and would not be completed until the time of Doge Giovanni Mocenigo (1478-1485). In 1483 a violent fire broke out in the side of the palace overlooking the canal, which housed the Doge's Apartments. Once again, important reconstruction work became necessary and was commissioned from Antonio Rizzo, who would introduce the new architectural language of the Renaissance into the building. An entirely new structure was raised alongside the canal, stretching from the Ponte della Canonica to the Ponte della Paglia. In 1485 the Maggior Consiglio ruled that a ceremonial staircase should be built within the palace courtyard. The design, again by Antonio Rizzo, envisaged this lying on a direct axis with the Foscari Arch, thus producing one single monumental approach from the piazza into the heart of the building. However, the following year the architect was accused of embezzlement and had to flee Venice; his place was taken by maestro Pietro Lombardo, who would oversee not only the completion of the Staircase but also the sculptural decoration of the façade. Work on the Doge's Apartments would finally end in 1510, whilst the official rooms of government were in this period decorated with works commissioned from such painters as Carpaccio, Giorgione, Alvise Vivarini and Giovanni Bellini. In 1515 Antonio Abbondi, known as Scarpagnino, would take over from Pietro Lombardo; and in the period of the Doge Andrea Gritti (1523-1538), Titian would work extensively on the decoration of various rooms in the building. Only in 1559 was the palace complete, with each organ of the state administration having its own rooms. In 1567 Sansovino's two colossal statues of *Neptune* and *Mars* were raised on the ceremonial staircase, which thereafter became known as the Scala dei Giganti. And thus this important phase of rebuilding work came to an end.

Jacopo Sansovino, Neptune, 1567. Venice, Doge's Palace, Scala dei Giganti.

*Antonio Da Ponte
and Antonio Contin,
The Prigioni Nuove, Venice.*

However another huge fire (in 1574) destroyed some of the rooms on the second floor of this wing, causing particular damage to the Sala della Quattro Porte, the Anticollegio, the Collegio itself and the Senato – fortunately, without undermining the structure as whole. Work on this refurbishment had hardly finished when another huge fire damaged the Sala dello Scrutinio and the Sala del Maggior Consiglio, destroying works by such artists as Gentile da Fabriano, Pisanello, Alvise Vivarini, Carpaccio, Bellini, Pordenone and Titian. Of all the various proposals for rebuilding work, that put forward by Giovanni Antonio Rusconi was the one finally accepted. This envisaged swift repairs that would maintain the original appearance of the palace, and in the years 1579-80 – when Nicolò da Ponte was doge – all the necessary work was completed. Up to this point, the Doge's Palace had housed not only the doge's apartments, the seat of government and the city's courtrooms, but also a jail (on the ground floor, to the left and right of the Porta del Frumento). It was only in the second half of the sixteenth century that Antonio da Ponte undertook the design of the Prigioni Nuove [New Prisons], completed by Antonio Contin around 1600 and linked to the palace itself by the

Ponte dei Sospiri. This transfer of the prisons left the old space on the ground floor of the Palace free, and at the beginning of the seventeenth century work began on restructuring the courtyard. In the wing that houses the courtrooms, a colonnade was created that was similar to that on the Renaissance façade opposite, whilst on the inner side (opposite the waterfront wing of the palace) a marble façade was constructed alongside the Foscari Arch. Designed by Bartolomeo Manopola, this is decorated with blind arches and surmounted by a clock (1615). For more than a thousand years, the Doge's Palace had been the heart and symbol of political life and public administration within the Venetian Republic. Hence when that Republic fell in 1797, its role inevitably changed (see p. 21). Venice was subjected first to French rule, then to Austrian, and ultimately (in 1866) became part of a united Italy. Over this period the Palace was occupied by various administrative offices as well as housing the Biblioteca Marciana (from 1811 to 1904) and other important cultural institutions within the city. By the end of the nineteenth century the structure was showing clear signs of decay, and the Italian government set aside sizeable funds for extensive restoration. It was then that many of the original capitals of the fourteenth-century arcade were removed and substituted; the originals now form the core of the collection in the Museo dell'Opera. What is more, all the public offices occupying the building were moved elsewhere, with the exception of the State Office for the Protection of Historical Monuments, which is still housed in the building. In December 1925 the Italian State, owner of the building, entrusted management of the palace to Venice City Council, laying down that it was to be run as a museum open to the public.

Venice, Doge's Palace. The north side of the courtyard.

Filippo Calendario (?),
The Drunkenness of Noah,
fourteenth century (detail).
Venice, Doge's Palace.
Sculptural group on the right
side of the waterfront façade.

The Exterior

The oldest extant part of the palace is the façade overlooking the waterfront, the corners of which are decorated with fourteenth-century sculptural groups that are attributed to Filippo Calendario and various Lombard artists such as the Raverti and the Bregno. On the corner next to the Ponte della Paglia, the groups depict *Archangel Raphael and Tobias* (above) and *The Drunkenness of Noah* (below); on the Piazzetta corner of the building, there is *Archangel Michael* (above) and *Adam and Eve* (below). On both the waterfront and Piazzetta sides of the palace, the ground-level arcade and the loggia above are decorated with fourteenth- and fifteenth-century capitals, some of which were replaced with copies during the nineteenth century (the originals can now be seen in the Museo dell'Opera). The central balcony on the waterfront façade dates from the beginning of the fifteenth century (1400-1404); designed by Pier Paolo Dalle Masegne, it fits in perfectly with the fourteenth-century architecture of the whole. The crowning part of the balcony was re-done in 1579, with Alessandro Vittoria's statue of *Justice* being raised in place of one that had collapsed during a 1511 earthquake. The statue of *St. George*, however, dates from the eighteenth century (the work of Giovanni Battista Pellegrini); the other figures are *St. Theodore*, *The Cardinal Virtues*, *St. Mark*, *St. Peter* and *St. Paul*. On the Piazzetta front of the building, there is an interesting bas-relief of *Justice Enthroned*, located above the thirteen column of the arcade between the quadrilobes of the loggia; the early-sixteenth-century balcony in the centre of the façade is based on that within the waterfront side of the building. The sculptural group at the corner before the Porta della Carta is an interesting composition, showing *The Judgement of Solomon*,

Alessandro Vittoria, statue
of Justice, *1579. Detail seen*
from the roof of the waterfront
wing of the palace.

Filippo Calendario (?), Eve, fourteenth century. Venice, Doge's Palace. Sculptural group on the left side of the waterfront façade.

*View of the Doge's Palace
seen from St. Mark's Basin and
the Piazzetta.*

with the *Archangel Gabriel* above; critics now tend to attribute this
to Bartolomeo Bon. It is more than likely that the three corner groups
were intended to symbolise the main characteristics of Venetian society,
and that the location of this composition here was meant to underline
the role of the palace as the seat of justice. In 1438-1442 Giovanni and
Bartolomeo Bon built and adorned the Porta della Carta, which served
as the ceremonial entrance to the building; on the architrave is the

*Giovanni and Bartolomeo Bon,
The Porta della Carta,
1438-1442. Venice, Doge's
Palace, Piazzetta façade.*

inscription *opus bartholomei*. The name of the gateway [*carta*=paper]
probably derives either from the fact that this was the area where
public scribes set up their desks, or from the nearby location of the
cartarum, the archives of state documents. Designed in the Flamboyant
Gothic style, this gateway is distinguished by the richness of its
sculptural and surface decoration, much of which was originally
painted and gilded. Flanked by Gothic pinnacles, with two figures of
the *Cardinal Virtues* per side (attributed to Antonio Bregno), the
gateway is crowned by a bust of *St. Mark* over which rises a statue of
Justice with her traditional symbols of sword and scales. In the space
above the cornice there is a sculptural portrait of Francesco Foscari,
doge at the time the gateway was built; he is shown kneeling before
the Lion of St. Mark. This is, however, a nineteenth-century work (by
Luigi Ferrari) raised to replace the original group destroyed in 1797
(a fragment can still be seen in the Museo dell'Opera). Nowadays, the
public entrance to the Doge's Palace is via the Porta del Frumento on
the waterfront side of the building, and it is there that our visit begins.

The itineraries through the museum do not proceed in a uniform direction from one floor to the next; organized according to theme they move backwards and forwards several times. The information panels and room numbers reflect this, with the visit proceeding from the magnificent rooms of the Doge's Apartments – on the first floor – to the Government and State Rooms on the second floor and the loggia floor. The visit ends at the Armoury and Prisons. There is also a Secret Itinerary tour, which is not included in the normal visit to the palace but has to be booked in advance; for details, apply at the Information Desk at the museum entrance.

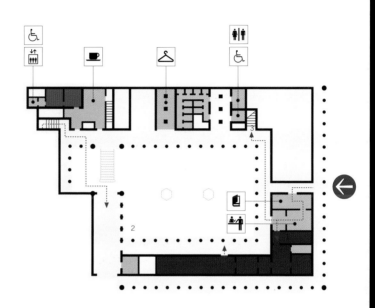

Entrance

1   Museo dell'Opera

2   Courtyard

3   Scala dei Censori

■ **Museo dell'Opera**

■ **Temporary Exhibitions**

■ **Areas of the Museum currently closed to the public**

■ **Public Facilities**

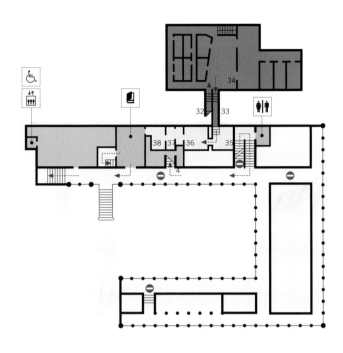

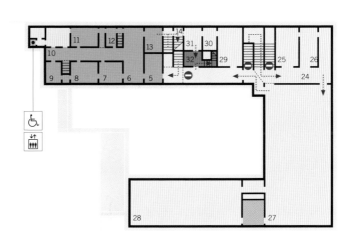

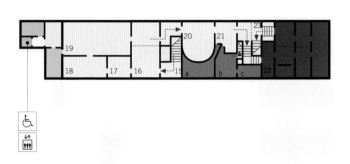

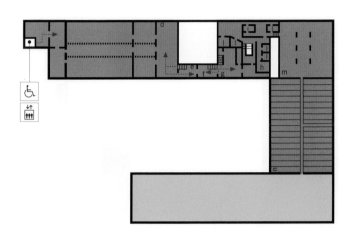

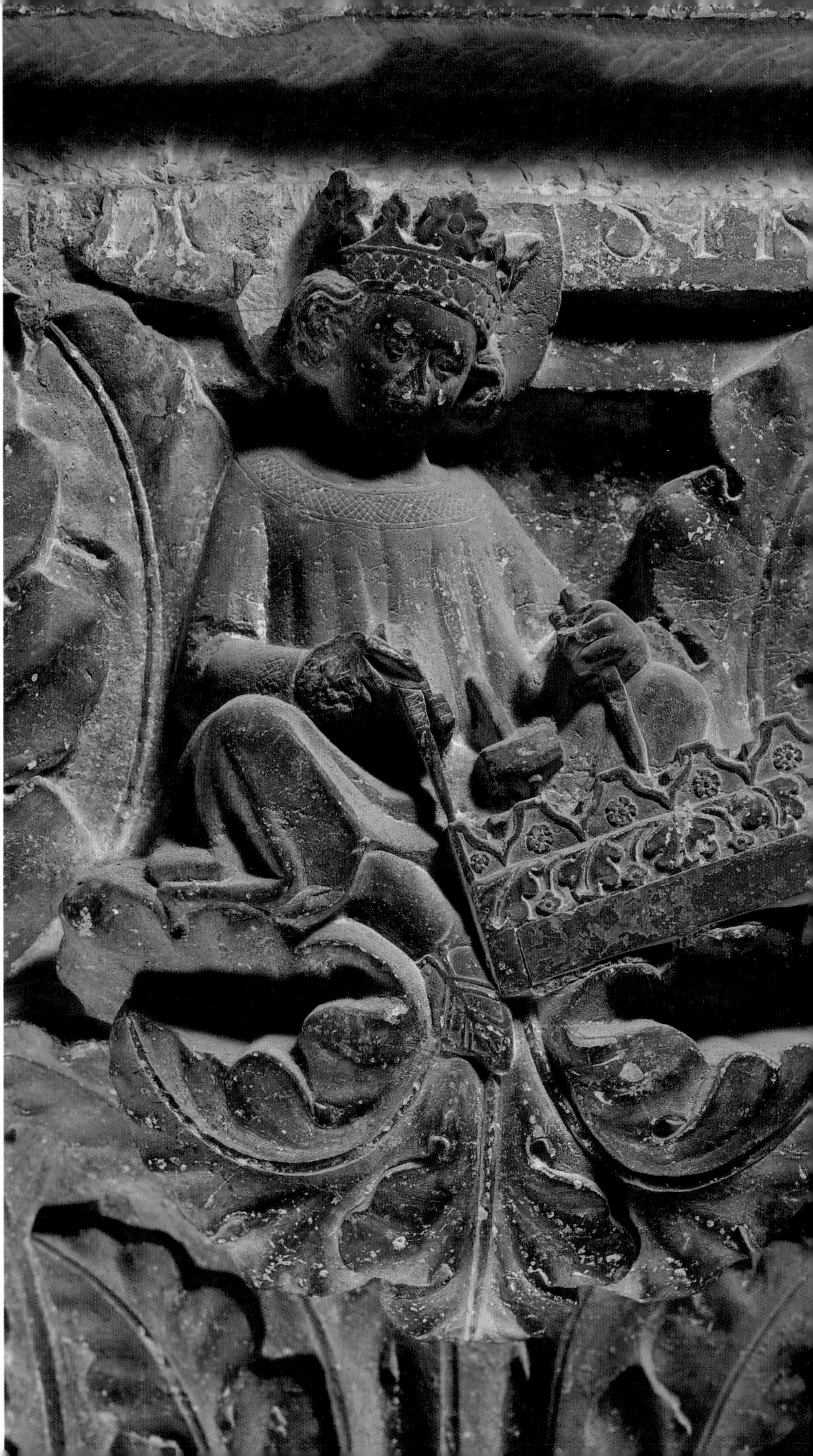

The Museo dell'Opera

Filippo Calendario (?), capital depicting Stone-cutter Saints and Disciples. *Detail with St. Nichostratus, fourteenth century. Venice, Doge's Palace, Museo dell'Opera, Room II.*

This Museo dell'Opera [Museum of the Palace Fabric] takes its name from the Opera – also known as the *fabbriceria* or *procuratoria* – which used to be the technical office responsible for the maintenance of the palace and the countless schemes of improvement and restoration that were implemented during the course of its long history. The present-day museum conserves documents and material that are a record of this activity. One of the most important restoration plans of modern times was launched in 1875, and involved both the façades of the building and the ancient capitals of the ground-floor arcade and the loggia: no fewer than 42 of these capitals, which were particularly old, valuable or fragile were replaced by copies at this time. The originals, which were stored in the palace, subsequently underwent careful restoration during the last decade of the twentieth century; at the same time, plans were drawn up to convert part of the area of the ground floor to create a Museo dell'Opera, which was intended to house these and other important architectural remains from the Palace. The capitals in the Museum are a valuable and important part of a remarkable collection of sculpture and carved reliefs that used to embellish the mediaeval façades of the Doge's Palace. More than simple decoration however, these works were inspired by complex allegorical, religious, moral and political ideas that were undoubtedly clearer to the people of the fourteenth and fifteenth century than they are to us.

Filippo Calendario (?), capital depicting The Creation of Adam and the Houses of the Planets, *fourteenth century. Detail with Jupiter. Venice, Doge's Palace, Museo dell'Opera, Room III.*

Crowded with men, women, children, animals, plants, signs of the Zodiac, symbols and allegories of vices and virtues, the dozens of sculpted capitals make up a veritable "poem" in stone; their conflation of fable, exemplum and moral tale reflects that typically-mediaeval practice of uniting the sacred and the profane, the historical and the mythical. The objects on display in the six rooms of Museo dell'Opera are accompanied by material that aims to enable visitors to "read" this encyclopaedic compendium of knowledge and parable.

Room I

The six capitals and columns in this room come from the palace's fourteenth-century waterfront arcade; they thus form part of the oldest extant sculptural decoration of the building, upon which work began in 1340. The first on the right depicts *Solomon and the Seven Wise Men*. The capital shows the Liberal Arts mastered by Solomon, who subjects pagan knowledge to the dominion of the Christian faith; the fact that he is shown studying two books reveals his care and prudence is consulting his sources. The figure in the large-buttoned tunic – on the side of the capital facing the wall – Solomon is to be interpreted as a representative of divine wisdom; the champion of a higher form of knowledge, he demonstrates his clear superiority over the Seven Wise Men (all of whom are shown sitting cross-legged in a position that was typical of the Eastern world and symbolized both power and meditation). Continuing in an anti-clockwise direction round the capital, the Seven Wise Men are: *Priscian*, who represents Grammar and is shown writing in a book; *Aristotle*, the incarnation of Dialectics, who is pointing at another book; *Cicero*, master of Rhetoric, who raises his right hand in the declamatory gesture of someone making a public address; *Pythagoras*, Arithmetic, who is aligning four objects – perhaps coins – on a tablet engraved with the number 1344, which may be the date when the capital was carved; *Euclid*, Geometry, using a pair of compasses; *Tubal*, credited with the invention of Music, who is shown playing a stringed instrument; and finally *Ptolemy*, the father of Astrology, who points at the sky with his finger. Behind this is a capital decorated with *Male heads of various races*. Rendered with great realism and skill by the anonymous sculptor, these busts represent the various peoples of the Earth.

To the right, behind the head of a bearded man, is that of a Moor wearing a turban. On the left is an elderly man on whose cap are two small Lions of St. Mark; he may therefore be an inhabitant of a land subject to Venice, perhaps Crete. Two more faces follow: the slanting eyes and snub nose of the second make it clear that he is intended to depict a Tartar.

Capital depicting Solomon with the Seven Wise Men, *fourteenth century. Detail with* Aristoteles Dialecticus. *Venice, Doge's Palace, Museo dell'Opera, Room I.*

Room II

Unlike the capitals in the previous room, the four in this room (with columns) were originally located on the façade overlooking the Piazzetta. Of remarkable quality, the sculptural decoration here is very rich in allegorical and moral significance, covering themes related to Work, the Fruits of the Earth and Astrology. The late-sixteenth-century curtain wall from one of the large arches in the arcade near the Ponte di Paglia is mounted on the entrance wall: after a great fire in 1577 it was decided to brick in these final arches in order to guarantee the stability of the building. The second capital on the right, which depicts various *Trades,* is particularly interesting. Whereas the capital in the previous room depicted the Liberal Arts, this one shows the Mechanical Arts that were practised inside and outside the city walls. The first trade or craft – viewing the capital with the doorway behind you – is that of the *stonecutter,* whose work was particularly important in the creation of the palace. Continuing in an anti-clockwise direction, there are: the *goldsmith,* whose activity was dignified by the richness of the raw materials used; the *cobbler;* the *carpenter;* the *measurer of cereals and pulses;* the *farmer;* the *notary,* and finally, the *blacksmith.* It is interesting to note that the hats they wear allow us to identify their status: the master craftsmen (the notary, the stonecutter and the goldsmith) wear a voluminous cap turned back to front; the wage-earning artisans (the carpenter and the smith) wear a bonnet, and the apprentices (the cobbler) are bare-headed.

Capital depicting Male Heads of Different Races, *fourteenth century (detail). Venice, Doge's Palace, Museo dell'Opera, Room I.*

Room III

This room houses three capitals with columns. The first on the left and
the first on the right date back to the fourteenth century, whilst the one
situated at the end is from the fifteenth century.

The first capital on the right, described by Ruskin as "the most
beautiful in Europe," was situated on the corner between the Piazzetta
and the waterfront, under the sculptural group depicting *Adam and
Eve*; its very position indicates the importance it had in the entire
decorative scheme of the palace. In fact, the scene – *The Creation
of Adam and the Houses of the Planets* – marks the start of the story of
humankind and the universe which then unfolds over the two façades
of the building. The reading of the capital – with your back to the
entrance doorway – begins with the Creation of Man, on the left, and
continues with the depiction of the planets and the signs of the Zodiac
corresponding to them. Seated on a throne, God is shown holding the
head and an arm of the Adam he has just created. Proceding anti-
clockwise, you come to *Saturn*, a bearded old man seated in the house
of Capricorn and holding the precious jug of Aquarius. It is also
possible to see the accompanying scythe as symbolizing his role

as protector of the workers in the fields and lord of man's last years and death. On the third side *Jupiter*, with a cape fastened at the neck 0and a scholar's cap, is shown touching the Sign of Pisces and sitting in the House of Sagittarius; he is armed with a bow and arrow. *Mars* follows in the guise of a warrior dressed in a suit of armour and armed with a sword and shield; he sits in the House of Aries with Scorpio at his side. A handsome youth whose head is encircled by rays occupies the fifth side. He is Apollo, seated in the House of Leo and holding up the sun in his left hand. *Venus*, on the sixth side, portrayed with a sash fastened at her breast, admires her beauty in a mirror as she sits in the House of Taurus holding Libra. Next to her is *Mercury*, dressed in a toga with an open book in his hand. He is situated between Virgo and Gemini. The final side is occupied by a girl in a boat who is holding up the crescent moon and touching a crab, the symbol of Cancer. The small ship and her flowing locks tossed by the wind recall the influence of the Moon on the tides and on the winds. At the far end of the room, the last capital depicts the *Seven Deadly Sins*. Viewed with your back to the entrance and proceeding in an anti-clockwise direction, these are: *Pride*, in the form of a warrior armed with sword, shield and the horned helmet of Satan; the aged figure of *Anger*, who tears at his clothes and curses the heavens; *Avarice*, who grasps two small bags in his clenched fists; and *Sloth*, imprisoned among branches in an indolent and passive pose. The next side is occupied by *Vanity*, which is included here though not actually one of the Seven Deadly Sins; this is symbolized by a girl whose head is adorned with flowers and who touches her breast as she admires herself in the mirror she holds in her lap. *Envy* follows, fuming with rage as she points at the young girl, who makes her fully aware that she herself is no longer the object of other people's desie. The snake that encircles her head and the dragon that she clasps to her breast underline her fiendish aspect. *Lust* bares a breast as she looks at herself in the mirror and finally *Gluttony* holds up a glass and raises a haunch of meat to his mouth.

Room IV

This room houses two column shafts from the arcade and a stout wall of huge, rough-hewn blocks of drystone, which dates back to an early phase in the history of the palace.

Room V

There are two more column shafts from the arcade lined up along the entrance wall, whilst the one placed on the adjacent wall, with the foliage capital, comes from the loggia of the Piazzetta façade. Part of the tracery of the loggia has also been mounted in this room, with a succession of capitals; the inflected pointed arches form quadrilobes that are surmounted by a cornice decorated with rosettes. In the spandrels between the arches are lions' heads.

Room VI

This room houses 29 capitals from the loggia. Compared to the capitals from the ground-floor arcade, these reveal a greater interest in decorative motifs: foliage prevails and the flattened, smaller figures blend in with the leaves. Although carved in a rougher, coarser manner, the images from the loggia also depict the Universe and the influence of the stars on the sublunary world. Various stone fragments from the façades are exhibited on the walls: pinnacles, small arches and columns, which were removed and replaced with copies because they were damaged or in a parlous state. At the far end of the room is the architrave of the Porta della Carta bearing the inscription with the name of the architect-stonemason: Bartolomeo Bon. Moving back along the right-hand wall, you come to a bust. It is all that remains of the group depicting the *Doge Cristoforo Moro with the Lion of St. Mark* which once stood in a niche opposite the Giants' Staircase and was demolished at the fall of the Venetian Republic in 1797. The group sculpted by Bartolomeo Bon to be placed above the lintel of the Porta della Carta – *Doge Francesco Foscari kneeling in front of the Lion of St. Mark* – also met the same fate. All that remains is the head of the doge, which can be seen on the same wall as you proceed towards the exit. The group currently placed above the Porta della Carta is a copy made in 1885.

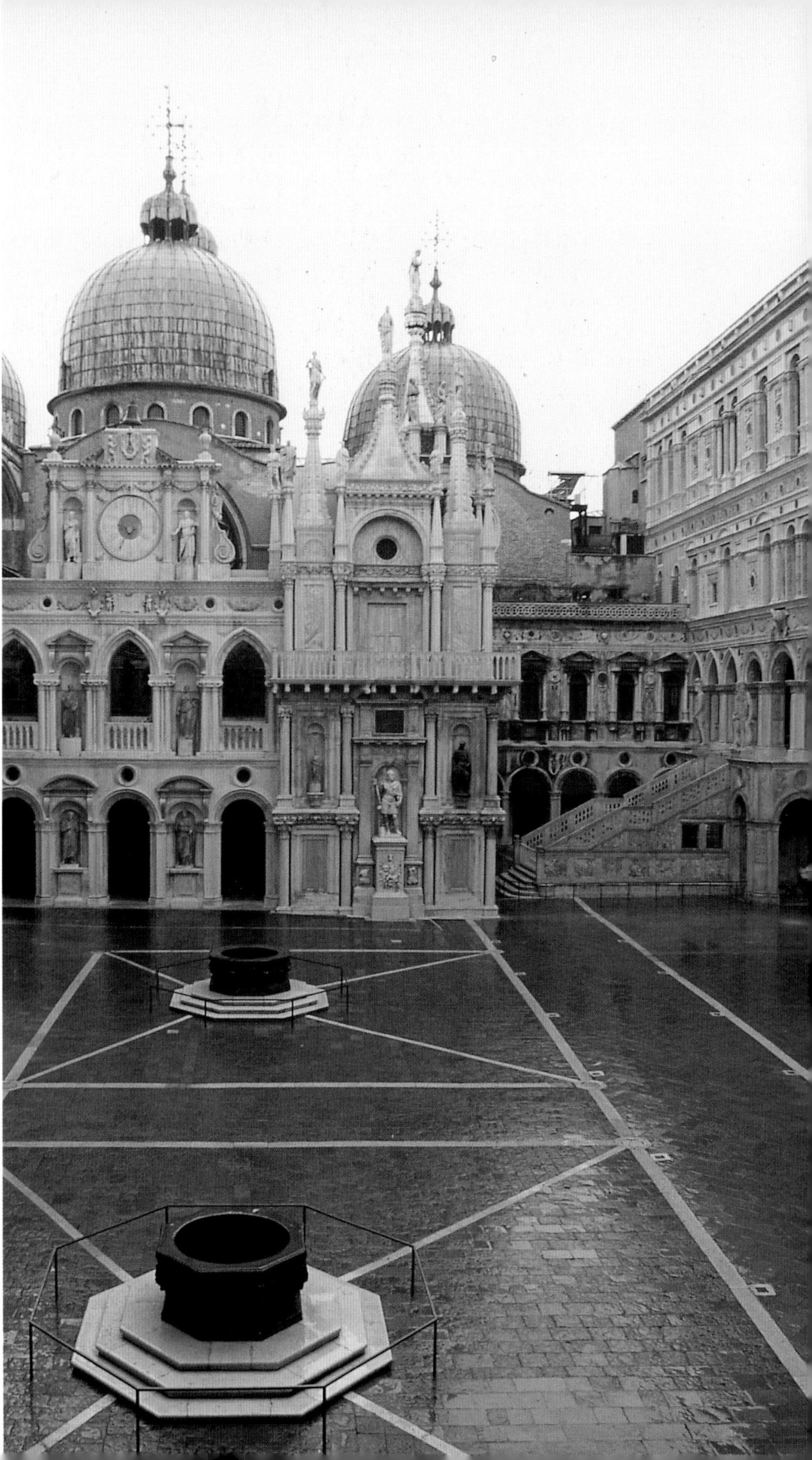

The Courtyard

The Courtyard

The courtyard of the Doge's Palace.

Visitors today enter the Doge's Palace by the Porta del Frumento in the oldest side of the building (that facing the waterfront). On your left (west) as you enter is the Piazzetta wing, whilst on the right (east) is the Renaissance wing. To the north – opposite you – the courtyard ends in the boundary between the palace and St. Mark's Basilica, which was the doge's chapel; the small marble façade with the clock (see p. 29) dates from the re-building work of 1615.

At the centre of the courtyard are two octagonal well-heads. Massive and highly-ornamental works in bronze, these were cast in the mid-sixteenth century by Nicolò de Conti and Albergeto; they differ from all other well-heads in the city not only in the material used but also in the richness of their bas-relief decoration.

The courtyard façade of the two oldest wings in the palace is rather simple and sever when compared to the wealth of decoration on the Renaissance wing; that side of the courtyard culminates in the Scala dei Giganti [Giants' Staircase] (see p. 27), decorated with bas-reliefs and with two colossal statues of *Neptune* and *Mars* (symbols of Venetian power by land and by sea). Near that Staircase is the rounded triumphal arch dedicated to Doge Francesco Foscari (1423-1457); in alternate bands of Istrian stone and red Verona marble, this is crowned by Gothic-style pinnacles and allegorical figures of the Arts by Antonio Bregno and other masters of the Lombard School. On the side of the arch looking towards the Staircase there are also two statues by Antonio Rizzo: *Adam*

Luca Carlevarijs, The Courtyard of the Doge's Palace, in Fabriche e Vedute di Venetia..., 1703. Venice, Museo Correr.

The Barbarigo coat-of-arms (Doge Marco Barbarigo, 1485-1486; Doge Agostino Barbarigo, 1486-1501).

The Donà coat-of-arms (Doge Francesco Donà, 1545-1553).

and *Eve*. These are, however, copies of the originals which can now be seen inside the palace. Beyond the Scala dei Giganti lies the sixteenth-century Cortile dei Senatori [Senators' Courtyard], where these members of the Venetian government would assembly before meetings. Thanks to the presence of the coats-of-arms of the various doges reigning at the time it is fairly easy to establish the date of work on the east façade: on the first capital in the corner of the Cortile dei Senatori is the crest of Marco Barbarigo (1485-1486), which is followed by that of his brother Agostino (1486-1501) above the seventh arch of the arcade after the Scala dei Giganti; finally, just a little beyond that, comes the coat-of-arms of Francesco Donà (1545-1553). At the opposite end of this façade – that is, closer to the palace entrance – you pass under the arcade to the wide Scala dei Censori [Censors' Staircase], which was built in 1525 and may have been designed by Scarpagnino. It is here that visitors pass up to the floors above.

Venice, Doge's Palace. The Foscari Arch.

Venice, Doge's Palace. The Scala dei Giganti.

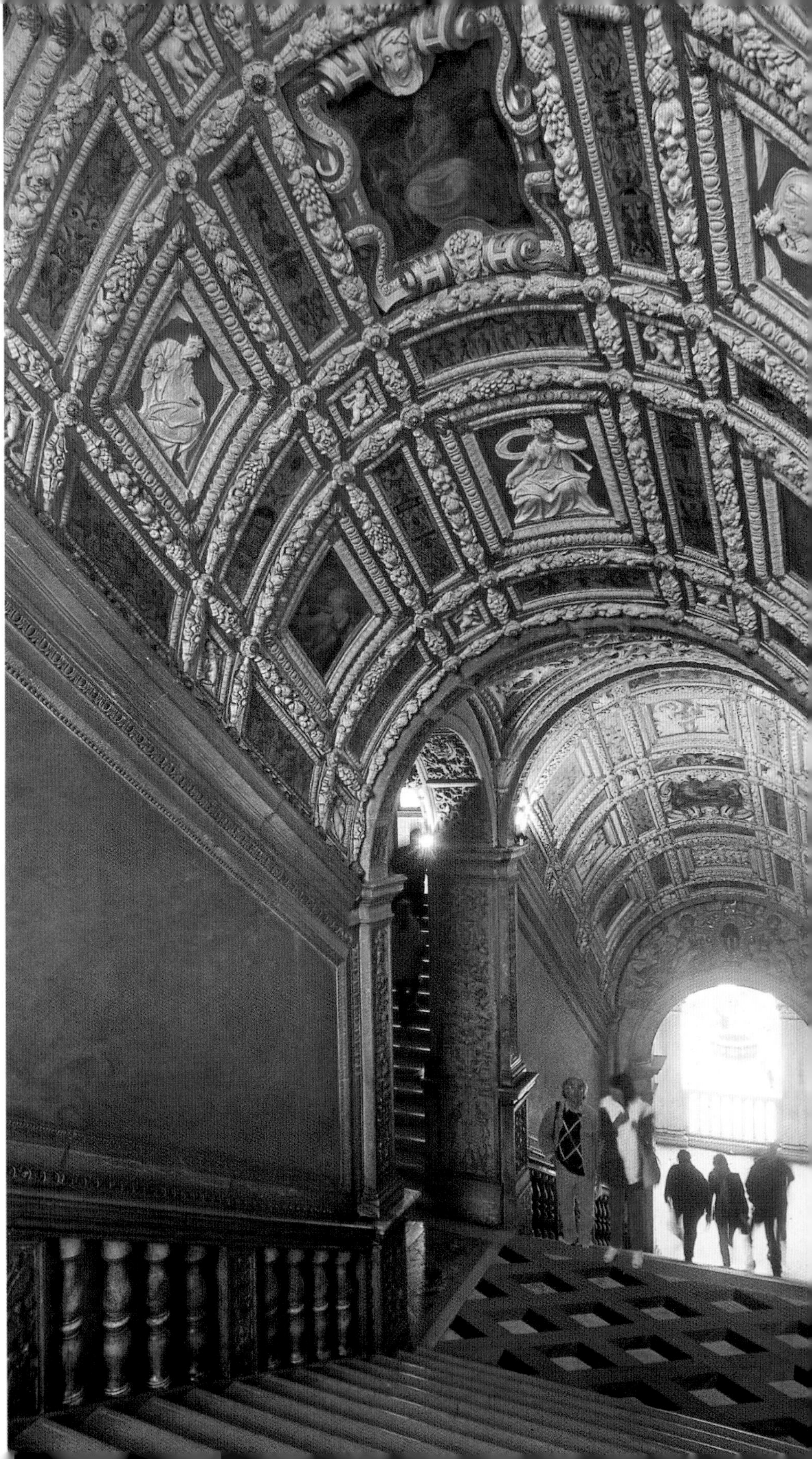

THE LOGGIAS AND THE SCALA D'ORO

The Scala d'Oro.

The first two flights of the Scala dei Censori bring you to the loggia overlooking the courtyard. This runs around three sides of the palace (east, south and west); and on the west side is paired with a loggia overlooking the Piazzetta. It is these arcades that make the mass of the palace strike one as so light and airy; nowadays, the loggia on this floor in the fourteenth-century wing houses the offices of the Venice Superintendence for the Environmental and Architectural Heritage, whilst in the Renaissance wing are the offices of the Venice Museum Authority and one of the bookshops within the palace. Originally, these rooms all housed different *magistrature* [government departments]. Set in the walls are various *bocche di leone* [lions' mouths], which from the end of the sixteenth century onwards were used by Venetians to "post" denunciations and accusations; on the other side of the wall was a box which opened directly into the office of the department or authority that was the intended recipient. It should, however, be pointed out that only rarely did the government act on such denunciations – and even then not without careful

The Winged Lion of St. Mark, seen from the loggia.

Bocca di Leone

These "lions' mouths" were located at various points in the Doge's Palace – for example, the walls of the loggia, in the Sala della Bussola and Sala della Quarantia Criminal. Through the open mouth of the lion, Venetians could slip secret denunciations of crimes and misdeeds. Each of the various *magistrature* [government departments] had its own bocca di leone.

confirmation of the facts. There are also two noteworthy plaques within the loggia on this floor. One, with an inscription in Gothic characters, dates from 1362 and bears Pope Urban V's promise of indulgences to those who give alms to prisoners. The other is opposite the head of the Scala dei Giganti and can be seen more easily at the end of the visit: a refined work by Alessandro Vittoria, it commemorates the visit to Venice by Henri III of France in 1574.

The Scala d'Oro

This "Golden Staircase" takes its name from the richness of its decorated vault, in white stucco and 24-carat goldleaf. This decor was the work of Alessandro Vittoria (from 1557 onwards), whilst the frescoed panels were painted in the same period by Giambattista Franco. The staircase was built at the behest of doge Andrea Gritti (his coat-of-arms can be seen on the arch) and design work began under Jacopo Sansovino in 1555, to be completed by Scarpagnino in 1559. Intended as the ceremonial approach to both the doge's private apartments and the main halls of government, this staircase is surmounted by two groups of marble statues. The work of Tiziano Aspetti (sixteenth century), these show, on the right, *Atlas holding up the Heavenly Vault*, and on the left, *Hercules Hilling the Hydra*. The dedication of the first flight of the Staircase to themes relating to Venus was an allusion to Venice's conquest of Cyprus, the island which was said to have been the goddess's birthplace. At the first landing, the staircase forks. It is the flight on the right which led to the doge's apartments. Again one can see how mythology served as a celebration of the Venetian Republic, because here the decoration is based on motifs relating to Neptune – a reference to Venice's dominion over the seas.

The word "doge" comes from the Latin *dux*; the title used for provincial governors within the empire of the East, this reflects the fact that up until the eighth century the peoples of the various lagoons in the Veneto recognized the formal sovereignty of Byzantium. Over the same period (seventh to ninth centuries) the city was withstanding incursions by the Longobards and the new Frankish empire, it also threw off subjection to the East. The result was that Venice became unique amongst the States of the day in that it recognized no source of sovereignty outside itself. Neither Guelph nor Ghibelline, it did not see its doge as invested in office by the authority of either the Pope or the Holy Roman Emperor; his investiture was an expression of the will of the people voting freely in a popular assembly.

Though there were attempts to transform this Commune into a dynastic regime – most notably, under the Candiano family in the tenth century – the unshakeable belief that sovereign power resided in "the people" continued to prevent the *Serenissimo Principe* from

Gentile Bellini,
Portrait of Doge Giovanni
Mocenigo, *1465-1479.*
Venice, Museo Correr.

ever becoming the master of the Republic (even if it is true that the political rights of "the people" were gradually restricted to an oligarchic group).

Elected by the Maggior Consiglio [Great Council], the plenary assembly of the Venetian nobility; watched over by his six Counsillors, who were inseparable from him in every minute of his public life; forced to submit every important decision to one of the great executive Councils of the Republic, the doge ultimately became a sort of father-figure for the State, an old gentleman whose "reign" crowned a career of service to Venice.

The only public figure who was appointed for life, he was to see his election as a reward for services rendered, not as a mandate for the exercise of his own initiative. Paradoxically, though he was the living symbol of the prestige of the Serenissima – receiving sovereigns and ambassadors, presiding over councils and tribunals – the doge was not even allowed to leave "his" palace without the permission of his "guardian angels."

More than a royal residence, the private apartments were a sort of gilded cage; the very provisional nature of the "tenant's" occupancy was underlined by the ritual looting that stripped the Palace clean of a deceased doge's personal effects. Apart from a few coats-of-arms and the name given to the odd room, almost nothing remains of the men who inhabited this building, sacrificing every instant of their private life to the solemn celebration of the glory of Venice.

Head of the councils of government and a participant at the highest levels of decision-making, the doge was nevertheless an embodiment of power. Not his own, but that of Venice itself.

As in all ancien regime States, the "spectacle of power" was the mainstay of popular consensus; and in Venice, the doge was central to the ideal image of authority and magnificence which the Republic projected through ceremonial and ritual.

"Most Serene Prince," the "King of Candy, of Cyprus and Morea," "Lord of a Half and of a Quarter of the Roman Empire" – these were just some of the titles that the doge could boast. They were an almost sacred embodiment of the power of the State – so solemn, in fact, that the man who bore them rose above personal ambition to become an impartial arbiter uninfluenced by faction.

The Doges

697-717	Paolo Lucio Anafesto	1148-1156	Domenico Morosini	1553-1554	Marcantonio Trevisan
717-726	Marcello Tegalliano	1156-1172	Vitale II Michiel		
726-737	Orso Ipato	1172-1178	Sebastiano Ziani	1554-1556	Francesco Venier
737-741	Periodo dei Magistri	1178-1192	Orio Malipiero	1556-1559	Lorenzo Priuli
	Militum	1192-1205	Enrico Dandolo	1559-1567	Girolamo Priuli
742-755	Teodato Ipato	1205-1229	Pietro Ziani	1567-1570	Pietro Loredan
755-756	Galla Gaulo	1229-1249	Jacopo Tiepolo	1570-1577	Alvise Mocenigo I
756-764	Domenico	1249-1253	Marino Morosini	1577-1578	Sebastiano Venier
	Monegario	1253-1268	Ranieri Zen	1578-1585	Nicolò Da Ponte
764-787	Maurizio Galbaio I	1268-1275	Lorenzo Tiepolo	1585-1595	Pasquale Cicogna
787-804	Giovanni Galbaio	1275-1280	Jacopo Contarini	1595-1605	Marino Grimani
804-810	Obelario Antenoreo	1280-1289	Giovanni Dandolo	1606-1612	Leonardo Donà
810-827	Agnello Partecipazio	1289-1311	Pietro Gradenigo	1612-1615	Marcantonio
827-829	Giustiniano	1311-1312	Marino Zorzi		Memmo
	Partecipazio	1312-1328	Giovanni Soranzo	1615-1618	Giovanni Bembo
829-836	Giovanni I	1329-1339	Francesco Dandolo	1618	Nicolò Donà
	Partecipazio	1339-1342	Bartolomeo	1618-1623	Antonio Priuli
836-864	Pietro Tradonico		Gradenigo	1623-1624	Francesco Contarini
864-881	Orso I Partecipazio	1343-1354	Andrea Dandolo	1625-1629	Giovanni Corner
881-887	Giovanni II	1354-1355	Marino Falier	1630-1631	Nicolò Contarini
	Partecipazio	1355-1356	Giovanni Gradenigo	1631-1646	Francesco Erizzo
887	Pietro I Candiano	1356-1361	Giovanni Dolfin	1646-1655	Francesco Molin
888-912	Pietro Tribuno	1361-1365	Lorenzo Celsi	1655-1656	Carlo Contarini
912-931	Orso II Partecipazio	1365-1368	Marco Corner	1656	Francesco Corner
932-939	Pietro II Candiano	1368-1382	Andrea Contarini	1656-1658	Bertucci Valier
939-942	Pietro Partecipazio	1382	Michele Morosini	1658-1659	Giovanni Pesaro
942-959	Pietro III Candiano	1382-1400	Antonio Venier	1659-1675	Domenico Contarini
959-976	Pietro IV Candiano	1400-1413	Michele Steno	1675-1676	Nicolò Sagredo
976-978	Pietro I Orseolo	1414-1423	Tommaso Mocenigo	1676-1684	Alvise Contarini
978-979	Vitale Candiano	1423-1457	Francesco Foscari	1684-1688	Marcantonio
979-991	Tribuno Menio	1457-1462	Pasquale Malipiero		Giustinian
	Memmo	1462-1471	Cristoforo Moro	1688-1694	Francesco Morosini
991-1008	Pietro II Orseolo	1471-1473	Nicolò Tron	1694-1700	Silvestro Valier
1008-1026	Ottone Orseolo	1473-1474	Nicolò Marcello	1700-1709	Alvise Mocenigo II
1026-1032	Pietro Centranico	1474-1476	Pietro Mocenigo	1709-1722	Giovanni Corner II
1032-1042	Domenico	1476-1478	Andrea Vendramin	1722-1732	Alvise Mocenigo III
	Flabanico	1478-1485	Giovanni Mocenigo	1732-1735	Carlo Ruzzini
1043-1070	Domenico Contarini	1485-1486	Marco Barbarigo	1735-1741	Alvise Pisani
1070-1084	Domenico Selvo	1486-1501	Agostino Barbarigo	1741-1752	Pietro Grimani
1084-1096	Vitale Falier	1501-1521	Leonardo Loredan	1752-1762	Francesco Loredan
1096-1102	Vitale I Michiel	1521-1523	Antonio Grimani	1762-1763	Marco Foscarini
1102-1118	Ordelaffo Falier	1523-1538	Andrea Gritti	1763-1778	Alvise Mocenigo IV
1118-1130	Domenico Michiel	1539-1545	Pietro Lando	1779-1789	Paolo Renier
1130-1148	Pietro Polani	1545-1553	Francesco Donà	1789-1797	Lodovico Manin

Anafesto	Tegalliano	Ipato	Gaulo	Monegario	Galbaio	Antenoreo	Partecipazio	Tradonico
Candiano	Tribuno	Orseolo	Memmo	Centranico	Flabanico	Contarini	Selvo	Falier
Michiel	Polani	Morosini	Ziani	Malipiero	Dandolo	Tiepolo	Zen	Gradenigo
Zorzi	Soranzo	Dolfin	Celsi	Corner	Venier	Steno	Mocenigo	Foscari
Moro	Tron	Marcello	Vendramin	Barbarigo	Loredan	Grimani	Gritti	Lando
Donà	Trevisan	Priuli	Da Ponte	Cicogna	Bembo	Corner	Erizzo	Molin
Valier	Pesaro	Sagredo	Giustinian	Morosini	Ruzzini	Pisani	Foscarini	Renier
Manin								

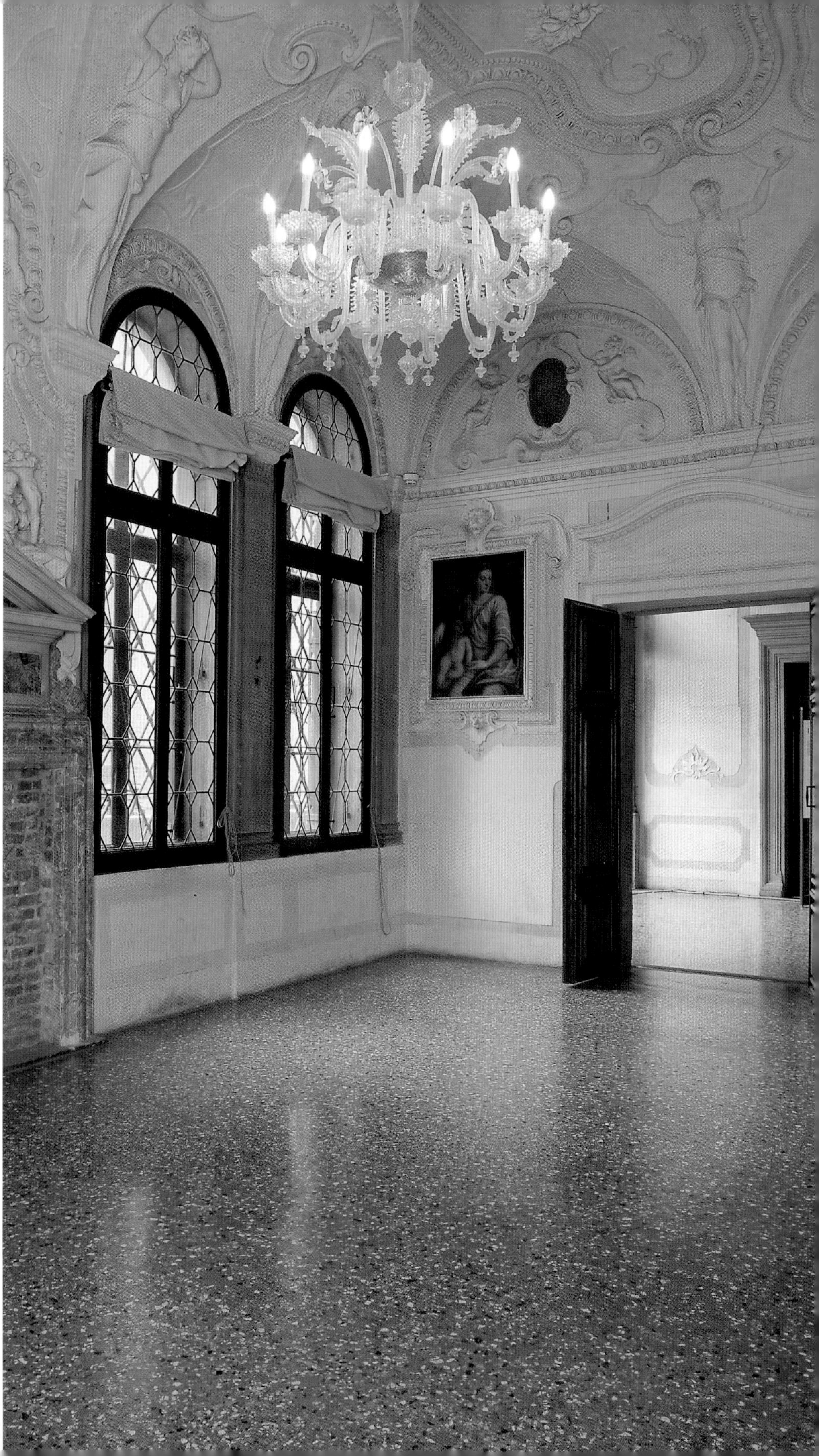

THE DOGE'S APARTMENTS

View of the Sala degli Stucchi.

The rooms of the doge's apartments were always situated in the area of the palace between the Rio della Canonica – the water approach to the building – the present site of the Scala d'Oro and the apse of St. Mark's (the doge's chapel). So, whilst undoubtedly prestigious, these ducal apartments were not vast, especially when one considers that the rooms closest to the Scala d'Oro were not reserved for strictly private use. After the 1483 fire (see p. 26) this wing was entirely rebuilt to designs by Antonio Rizzo and Pietro Lombardo, and must have been inhabitable by 1492. The doge's apartments were unfurnished as each doge was expected to bring furnishings from his own home; after his death, these were returned to his heirs.

The Sala dello Scudo

The name of this room comes from the fact that the coat-of-arms [*scudo*] of the reigning doge was exhibited here whilst he granted audiences and received guests. The coat-of-arms currently on display is that of Ludovico Manin, the doge reigning when the Republic of St. Mark came to an end in 1797.

The rotating globes in the Sala dello Scudo.

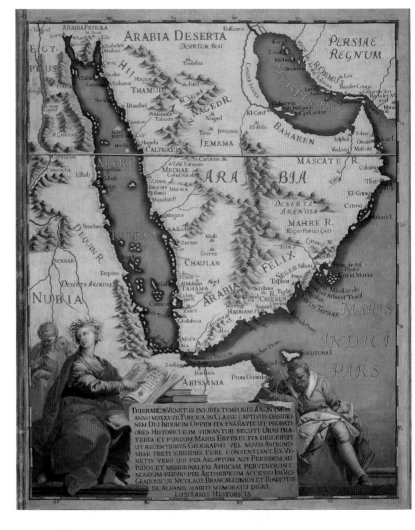

Francesco Grisellini and Giustino Menescardi, Arabia, 1762, Sala dello Scudo.

This is the largest and most airy room in the doge's apartments, and runs the entire width of this wing of the palace, from the canal to the courtyard; in a sense, it is the continuation at right angles of the so-called Sala dei Filosofi, forming that T shape which was a typical feature of the most traditional Venetian interiors.

The room was used as a reception chamber, and its decoration with large geographical maps was designed to underline the glorious extent of Venetian power. The original versions of these maps were produced after the 1483 fire by the geographer and humanist Giovan Battista Ramusio (Italy and the Mediterranean), the Greek Giovanni Domenico Zorzi (Asia Minor) and the Piedmontese cartographer Giacomo Gastaldi (Turkey, Egypt and the Asia of Marco Polo).

Adorning the two main walls of the room, these four geographical maps were re-worked in 1762 by the cartographer and polygraph Francesco Grisellini, who was commissioned by the scholar-doge Marco Foscarini to add other paintings that described the voyages of the most famous Venetian explorers: Nicolò and Antonio Zen, who travelled as far as Greenland; Pietro Querini, who was shipwrecked in the fjords of Norway; and Alvise da Mosto, who discovered the Cape Verde Islands.

The two revolving globes in the centre of the room date from the same period; one shows the sphere of the heavens, the other the surface of the Earth.

The Sala Grimani

This room takes its name from the Grimani armorial bearings to be seen in the centre of the ceiling. This powerful family supplied the Republic with three doges: Antonio (1521-1523), an authentic self-made man who had acquired a fortune through trade with the

View of the Sala Grimani.

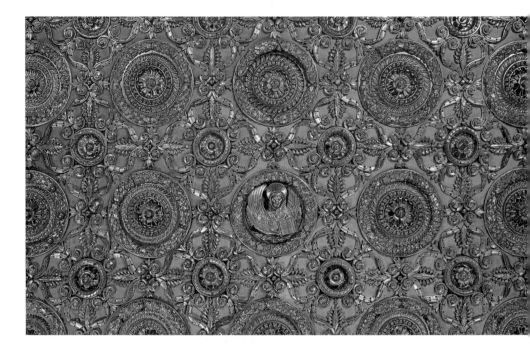

Orient; Marino (1595-1605), a cultured man who was not only
a patron of the arts but also a generous giver of alms to the poor;
and Pietro (1741-1752), a friend of Newton, from whom he learnt
a profitable lesson in the application of the English economic model.
The doge who had the magnificent ceiling created in this chamber
was certainly Marino.

Note the fireplace, which can be attributed to the workshop of the
Lombardo family and is decorated with the armorial bearings of
doge Agostino Barbarigo (1486-1501).

The elegant decorative band shows the Lion of St. Mark joyously
encircled with gods, goddesses and marine figures; the stucco-work
over the coping dates from the period of doge Pasquale Cicogna
(1585-1595).

The paintings in the frieze are all the work of Andrea Vicentino,
who produced them towards the end of the sixteenth century; the
allegorical figures are rather difficult to identify, with the exception
of: *St. Mark with the Lion*; *Geography*; *Agriculture*; *Law, Architecture*;
a female figure symbolising Venice; *Astronomy, Reward and the Virgin*.
On the walls is a collection of some of the most significant paintings
of the Lion of St. Mark: one by Jacobello del Fiore (signed and dated
1415); one by Donato Veneziano (1495) and the famous *Lion of
St. Mark* by Vittore Carpaccio (1516, see pp.18-19). In the latter,
the front paws on the earth and the back paws on the sea symbolise
the Republic's position as both a land and naval power.

The Sala Erizzo

This owes its name to Francesco Erizzo, doge from 1631 to 1646. Its decor includes a carved ceiling, with gilding against a blue background, and a Lombard-School fireplace surmounted by a coping, with the Erizzo coat-of-arms carved between the figures of Venus and Vulcan. Around the walls is a freize with putti and symbols of war which refer to the military achievements of doge Erizzo. On the walls hang paintings by Gerolamo Bassano (1566-1621) depicting episodes from the Life of Christ.

The Sala degli Stucchi, also known as the Sala Priuli

The stucco-work on the vault and the lunettes dates from the time of doge Marino Grimani (1595-1605), but the coat-of-arms on the fireplace is that of the Priuli family (doge Lorenzo, 1556-1559; Girolamo, 1559-1567; and Antonio 1618-1623). A later Grimani – Pietro (doge, 1741-1752) – would commission the stucco-work on the walls and ceiling in 1743, when the room was used to house the works left to the Republic by the nobleman Bertuccio Contarini. There are also paintings of various episodes from the Life of Christ – six by Giuseppe Salviati (1520-1575) and one by Leandro Bassano (1577-1622) – as well as a portrait of Henri III of France, which may be by Jacopo Tintoretto; this king received a magnificent reception in Venice in 1574 as he was making his way from Poland to take up the throne left vacant by the death of his brother, Charles IX.

Sala degli Stucchi, detail of the decoration.

*Titian, St. Christopher,
1523-1524. Sala dei Filosofi,
passageway leading
up to the second floor.*

The Sala dei Filosofi

At right-angles to the Sala dello Scudo, this long, narrow room owes
its name to the fact that it once housed twelve portraits of *Ancient
Philosophers* painted by Veronese and others in the second half
of the sixteenth century; initially intended for the Library Hall of the
Biblioteca Marciana, they were moved here at the behest of the
scholar-doge Marco Foscarini (1762-1763) and would remain in the
room until 1929, when they were replaced by the allegorical figures
one sees now. The stucco work also dates from the period of doge
Foscarini.

In the wall on the left (seen in relation to the Sala degli Stucchi)
there is a small doorway that leads to a narrow internal staircase that
gave the doge rapid access to his private apartments and the rooms
above, where the Senate and the Collegio met. On the wall above
the door is an important fresco by the young Titian (1523-1524) –
St. Christopher, a subject that was rich in symbolic significance.
Commissioned by doge Andrea Gritti just after his election, the
work was completed in just three days; significantly, the artist chose
to show the saint not crossing the traditional river but the lagoon
of Venice itself (in the background one can see the bell-tower,
the cupolas of the basilica and the Doge's Palace, with the mountains
beyond shown to the left).

St. Christopher was not only one of the so-called "auxiliary saints" –
whose help was called upon in cases of special necessity –
but also a convert who had been able to change the very meaning
of his life. The presence of the figure here – above a threshold –
could be taken to symbolize the desire to overcome the distinction
between the doge's public function and his existence
as a private individual.

The Sala Corner and Sala dei Ritratti

These two adjoining rooms had no specific function; part of the
private apartments of the doge, they might be used in different ways
to meet the needs of the new tenant and his family. Without any of
the original furnishings – apart from the magnificent fireplaces –
these rooms now house paintings of various provenance. In the first,
the paintings depict episodes from the life of doge Giovanni Corner
(1625-1629), whilst in the second – la Sala dei Ritratti – works
include: a *Madonna and Child Enthroned* by Alvise Vivarini; a Giotto-
school *Virgin at Prayer*; and the *Lament of the Dead Christ*, an intense
work painted (probably around 1472) by Giovanni Bellini in
collaboration with his brother Gentile.

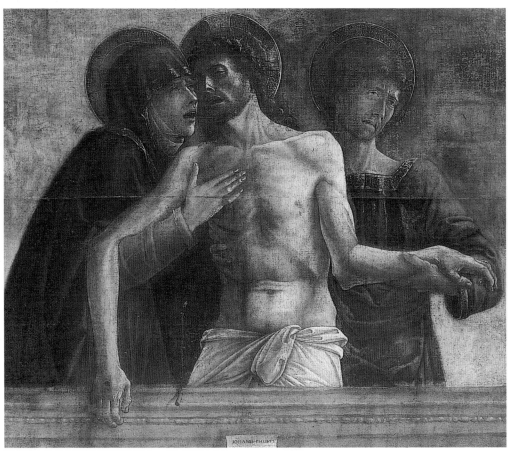

Giovanni Bellini, Lament of the Dead Christ, *1472. Sala Corner. Note the signature "JOHANNES BELLINUS."*

The Sala degli Scudieri

The *scuderi* [equerries] who gave this room its name were appointed for life by the doge, and eight of them had to be on duty at all times. Their various duties ranged from those of an equerry proper to those of standard-bearers who carried the symbols of the doge's power in public processions. The main entrance to the private apartments, this room no longer has its original decor, though it has preserved two fine doorways: one leading into the Sala dello Scudo, the other onto the landing of the Scala d'Oro. From this room, the modern-day visitor passes up the second flight of that Staircase to the chambers that housed the various governing councils of the Venetian Republic.

The landing of the Scala d'Oro seen from Sala degli Scudieri.

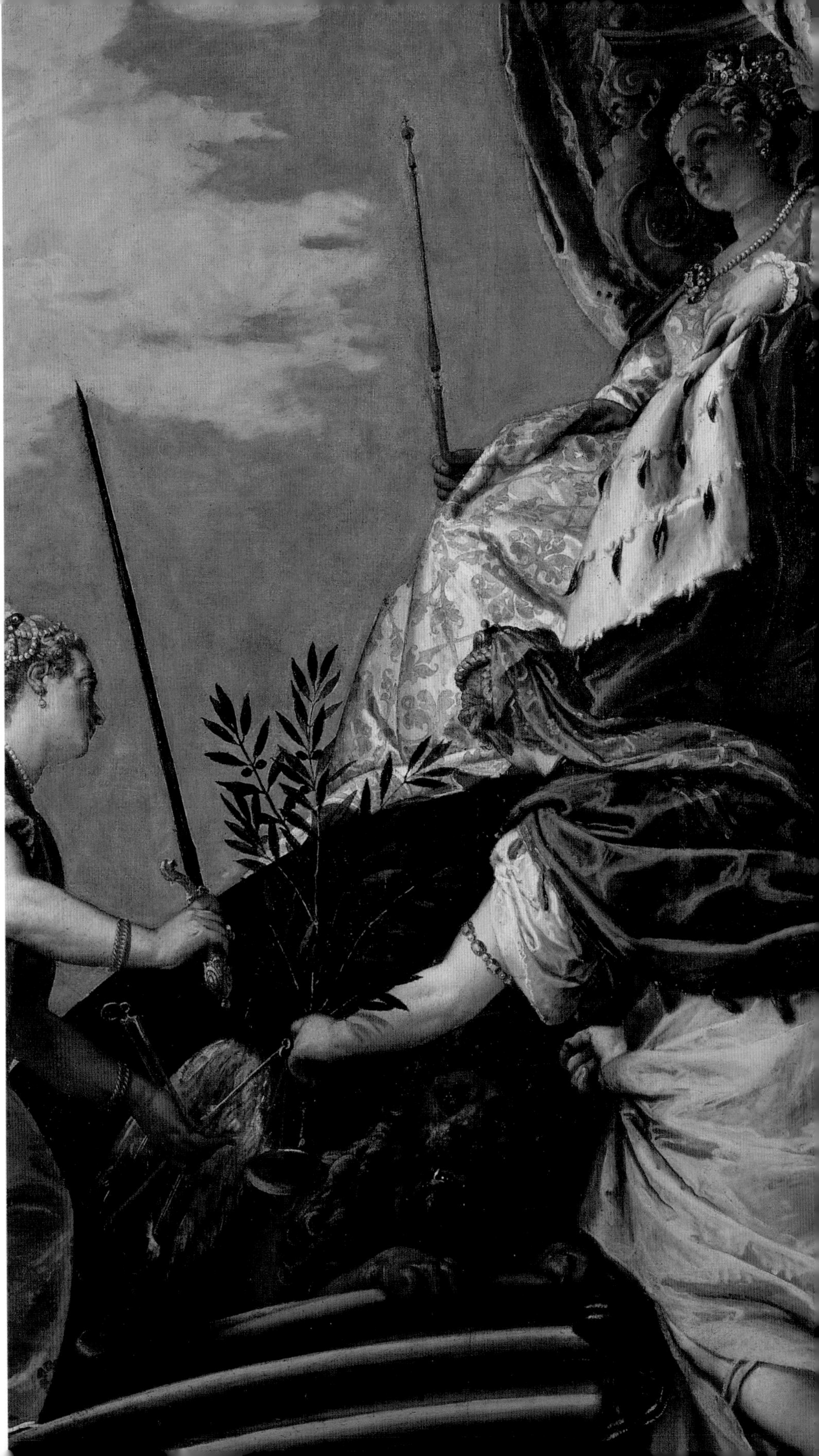

The Chambers of Government

Paolo Caliari, known as Veronese, Venice Enthroned with Peace and Justice, 1575-1578. Sala del Collegio, ceiling.

The second flight of the Scala d'Oro forms an imposing approach to the next floor of the palace, which houses the chambers of the councils that comprised the legislative, executive and judicial core of the Republic (the separation of these three functions was unknown in *Ancien Regime* States). Lavishly decorated – in order to impress visiting princes, prelates and ambassadors with the wealth and prestige of Venice – these rooms were where the Consiglio Ducale, the Signoria, the Senate, the Collegio and the Consiglio dei Dieci used to assemble and grant audiences. Elected by the Maggior Consiglio, which nevertheless maintained for itself the final say in important or controversial matters, these magistracies were responsible for the administration of justice, public finances and issues relating to internal and external security – all matters that could not have been handled efficiently by an assembly of 1,000-1,500 individuals.

In theory, access to these councils was open to every member of the Maggior Consiglio, but it is a fact that major responsibilities required experience – and that money could determine the outcome of many votes. Despite the rule that forbade the same person to occupy any office for more than a few months, an "inner circle" of figures ended up monopolizing most of the government positions. In each generation, no more than three hundred such individuals, who combined proven political skill with a solid "name" and fortune, alternated within the various councils.

However, it was not an entirely closed circle. The struggle to gain access to power was the very stuff of Venetian political life; and on more than one occasion, after a military setback or an economic crisis, the Maggior Consiglio did not hesitate to appoint entirely new councils.

The layout of the Chambers of government , which took on its final form after the serious fire that devastated this area of the palace in 1574, reflects the functions and needs of the magistracies that occupied them. One entrance, the Atrio Quadrato, gives onto the great state antechamber, known as the Sala delle Quattro Porte. Here, those awaiting an audience would be suitably impressed by the scurrying activity of clerks and secretaries, and might then reflect upon the greatness of a Republic whose diplomatic and military triumphs were depicted in the paintings on the walls.

The two doors opposite lead into the so-called 'aulic' chambers, which were directly linked to the doge's apartments by an inner staircase. That on the left leads into the Anticollegio, where the most distinguished foreign dignitaries would wait to be received in great state by the doge and his Collegio. That on the right leads into the Senate; a small assembly to which the Maggior Consiglio might delegate its authority, this was regularly attended by the most important civil and military figures in the State. The last of the four doors in the Sala delle Quattro Porte provided access to body that was much more private and expeditious in its exercise of power: the so-called Consiglio dei Dieci [Council of Ten]. Linked directly with the prisons, this room had its own ante-chamber, the Sala della Bussola, which was approached via the Scala dei Censori and the Armoury. For the most part, those seated there were not awaiting an audience but dreading an interrogation, whilst the Ten's own guards kept their beady eye upon them.

Atrio Quadrato
Continuing up the Scala d'Oro to the second floor, you come to the Atrio Quadrato [Square Atrium].
This is a fairly small chamber that serves as a hallway to the great Chambers of Government. The decoration was completed in the mid-sixteenth century under doge Gerolamo Priuli (1559-1567), whose portrait on the ceiling was painted by Jacopo Tintoretto (1564-1565); it is flanked by biblical scenes and putti by artists of the school of Tintoretto. During the dogeship of Priuli, the walls were adorned with four other canvases by the artist which are now

Jacopo Robusti, known as Tintoretto, Doge Girolamo Priuli receiving the Sword and Scales of Justice, 1565-1567.
Square Atrium, ceiling.

in the Sala dell'Anticollegio. In their place are other sixteenth-century works. The *St. John Writing the Book of Revelations* and an *Angel Appearing to the Shepherds* are ascribed by scholars to Paolo Veronese and Gerolamo Bassano respectively, whilst the *Expulsion of Adam and Eve from Eden* is more tentatively attributed to Veronese (or Paolo Fiammingo) and *Christ Praying in the Garden of Gethsemane* is by his school.

Sala delle Quattro Porte

The next room is the Sala delle Quattro Porte. An anteroom to the other chambers, it extends the whole width of this wing of the palace and was formerly the venue for meetings of the Collegio before becoming the domain of ushers. The four doors that give the room its name date from the 1483 restructuring, as do the multi-light windows giving onto the Rio di Canonica and the inner courtyard (the columned doorways themselves and statue-crowned lintels date from later). The decor was subsequently altered at various times and finally completely renewed after the fire of 1574. The commission for the new design was given to Andrea Palladio and Giovanni Rusconi, and the work was executed by Antonio da

View of the Sala delle Quattro Porte.

Ponte. A perfect example of the refined taste of the period, the barrel-vault ceiling is decorated with white stucco and gilding, and is attributed to Bombarda (1575-1577). Painted between 1578 and 1581, the frescoes on the ceiling are by Tintoretto but are based on an iconographical scheme drawn up by Francesco Sansovino. The circular panels represent *Juno Offering Venice the Peacock and Thunderbolt* and *Venice Breaking the Chains of Captivity*; the one in the centre represents *Venice Symbolically Receiving Dominion over the Adriatic from Jupiter*; while the eight ovals depict the cities and regions of the mainland (*Verona, Istria, Brescia, Padua, Friuli, Treviso, Vicenza, Altino*). The ovals of the lunettes represent *Philosophers*. The four portals, designed by Palladio, are surmounted by groups of sculpture alluding to the chamber into which they lead. The wall decoration, perhaps begun by Titian in the mid-sixteenth century, was completed later (1595-1600) under Doge Marco Grimani. The

Giambattista Tiepolo,
Neptune offering Venice the
Wealth of the Seas, *1740.*
Sala delle Quattro Porte.

canvases represent *Doge Antonio Grimani Kneeling before Religion and St. Mark* (begun by Titian and completed by his nephew Marco Vecellio); *The Venetians Conquer Verona* (by Giovanni Contarini); *The Legates of Nuremberg Receive the Laws of Venice from Doge Loredan* (by Carlo and Gabriele Caliari); *Henry III Arrives at Venice, Welcomed by the Doge and Patriarch* (by Andrea Vicentino); and *Doge Pasquale Cicogna Grants An Audience to the Persian Ambassadors* (by Carlo and Gabriele Caliari). On an easel stands *Venice Rising Above the World* (by Nicolò Bambini). Another work on an easel is Giambattista Tiepolo's *Neptune Offering Venice the Wealth of the Sea* (1740). This was painted to replace Tintoretto's *Venice Wed by Neptune, Who Makes Her Queen of the Seas*, which was originally situated above the windows facing the canal but became badly damaged by humidity. Now the painting by Tiepolo is not situated between the windows but is placed on an easel.

Venice and the Sea

Every year, on the Feast of the Ascension, there was the ceremony
in which the doge "married" the sea – a solemn reaffirmation of that
bond of union and domination between Venice and the Mediterranean,
the sea to which the city owned its existence, its safety and its wealth.
Devoid of towers, walls and castles, Venice was protected by the sea
itself, and during one thousand years of history it was never besieged
or occupied by its many enemies. The city also looked to the sea for
its livelihood, becoming the key to trade between the East and the
West – and amassing prodigious wealth for itself in the process. By the
twelfth century the city had established unchallenged control over the
Adriatic – the "Gulf of Venice" – and thereafter the Republic began to
create a veritable empire throughout the Mediterranean. This
comprised islands, naval bases, coastal fortresses and enfranchised
trading stations – all with one main purpose: the protection of
shipping routes for Venetian trade. Every year the *mude* (trading fleets)
would set off eastwards (to Alexandria, Beirut and Constantinople) and
westwards (to France, Spain, Flanders and England). These fleets were
organised by the Senate itself, which had the ships built and fitted out
in the Arsenale and then leased cargo space to individual merchants –
a public system that guaranteed a level of efficiency and safety that
would have been beyond the resources of private ship-owners. The
well-serviced routes of the Venetian *mude* became the channels along
which flowed the wealth of Mediterranean commerce. A leading role
in that trade – and in Mediterranean sea-craft in general – was played
by the Venetian galley; an oared vessel that could be used as a warship
or cargo carrier, this was particularly suited to coastal waters and
organisation in fleets. Contrary to what is generally believed, until well
into the sixteenth century the oarsmen were not slaves or prisoners,
but volunteers who signed up for pay and a minuscule – though
profitable – share of the cargo space, in which they could transport
goods for trade in the different ports of call. Commanded by such
figures as Sebastiano Ziani, Enrico Dandolo and Francesco Morosini
(whose surnames also figure amongst those of doges), Venetian war
galleys defended the martial glory of the Republic and were always in
the front-line in the interminable struggle between Christian Europe
and the Ottoman Empire. The "generator" behind so much power was
the Arsenale, which for centuries remained the largest industrial
establishment in the world. Compared by Dante to an infernal pit,

these state workshops were veritable production lines, capable of turning out some fifty galleys a month. In the sixteenth century, out of a city population of 150,000, more than 3,000 were *arsenalotti*, skilled workers who were the aristocracy of Venetian craftsmen and provided the core of popular consensus behind the government on which they depended for a living.

Allegorical statues at the entrance to the Arsenale, end of seventeenth century.

Sala dell'Anticollegio

The Sala dell'Anticollegio was an anteroom for ambassadors and delegations waiting to be received by the Venetian State.

The original decoration was destroyed in the fire of 1574. The room was restored first by Palladio and then Scamozzi.

The central fresco, *Venice Conferring Rewards and Honours*, is by Paolo Veronese. On the wall with the windows there is a chimney-piece in Palladian style, with statues by Scamozzi; the upper relief is by Tiziano Aspetti. The walls, up to 1716 covered with precious hangings, were later adorned with paintings.

On either side of the door are the four canvases Tintoretto originally painted for the Sala delle Quattro Porte: *Mercury and the Graces*, *Minerva Driving Away Mars, Ariadne Found by Bacchus* and *Vulcan's Forge*. These works have been interpreted as an allegory of the wise government of the Venetian Republic or, with greater probability, the harmonious succession of the seasons, identified with the harmony of good government.

The latter explanation seems to be corroborated by the putti representing the seasons in the previous room, the original location of the paintings. On the wall opposite the window are the *Rape of Europa* by Paolo Veronese and the *Return of Jacob with his Family* by Jacopo da Ponte, known as Bassano.

Access to the following room is through a doorway with a marble group attributed to Alessandro Vittoria.

View of the Sala dell'Anticollegio.

*Jacopo Robusti, known
as Tintoretto,* Ariadne found
by Bacchus, *1576.
Sala dell'Anticollegio.*

Paolo Caliari, known as Veronese,
Rape of Europa, *1576-1580. Sala
dell'Anticollegio.*

Sala del Collegio

The Sala del Collegio was intended for assemblies of the magistracy known as the Pien Collegio, which was made up of the Signoria [the Minor Consiglio], the three Capi della Quarantia [Heads of the Tribunals of Forty] and the three Zonte [the Savi del Consiglio, Savi di Terraferma and Savi degli Ordini]. In this chamber they received ambassadors, and it was therefore necessary for it to be particularly splendid. The room's structure, the main features of which were established soon after 1483, was completed with the present decorations after the fire of 1574, when it was rapidly redecorated following a project by Palladio, perhaps with the collaboration of Rusconi; the wooden wainscoting and carved ceiling are by Francesco Bello and Andrea Faentin (1576) and the splendid paintings on the ceiling by Veronese (1575). We know that work on the room was complete on the death of Doge Venier (1578), and the fact that the decoration was completed so swiftly certainly helped to confer on the chamber its distinctive unity of design. The wooden benches and dais are original and hence quite different to those in the other rooms, nearly always much later work; the dossals, however, are of a later date, replacing those destroyed in the fire of 1574. The very fine chimney-piece between the windows is by Gerolamo Campagna (1585-1595). The cycle of paintings on the

Paolo Caliari, known as Veronese, Mars and Neptune, 1575-1578. Sala del Collegio, ceiling.

Paolo Caliari, known as Veronese, Arachne or Dialectics, *1575-1578.* Sala del Collegio, ceiling.

Sala del Collegio, the throne.

ceiling is intended to extol the power and glory of Venice: the central compartments represent *Mars and Neptune*; *Faith, the Strength of the Republic* and *Venice Enthroned with Justice and Peace*, works that can be confidently ascribed to Veronese.

At the sides are depicted the *Virtues*, each with its symbolic attribute. Above the dais is a painting that represents *The Redeemer Venerated by Sebastiano Venier and Saints*, also by Veronese.

The walls are decorated with works by Tintoretto and his workshop (1581-1584): of particular interest is *Doge Andrea Gritti Worshipping the Virgin*, in which the master's hand seems evident.

Sala del Senato

The Sala del Senato was also known as the Sala dei Pregadi because its members were invited (*pregati*) in writing to attend council meetings. The term Senato appeared in documents only at the end of the fourteenth century, when the number of members was fixed at sixty.

The Serrata [closure] of the Maggio Consiglio in 1297 severely pruned its powers, but the patricians, hostile to the idea of creating another political organ, restored to the Senate its original political powers. The number of members increased rapidly in the sixteenth century thanks to the incorporation of the Quarantia [Tribunal

Clock with Zodiac (detail). Sala del Senato.

of Forty], Consiglio dei Dieci and a Zonta composed of sixty members, so that by the middle of the sixteenth century there were about 300 Senators. The Senate meetings were also attended by the doge and his councillors as well as magistrates; it dealt mainly with political issues and also decided on declarations of war and special appointments.

The Sala del Senato was used for meetings of the Senate, the most ancient institution in the Venetian State. We have, unfortunately, little information about the original decoration of the chamber, destroyed in the fire of 1574. Renovation in this room began some years later than in the others, with Antonio da Ponte being commissioned to do the work during the "reign" of Pasquale Cicogna; that doge's coat-of-arms are carved among the decorations in the ceiling, which was the work of Cristoforo Sorte (1580s). Soon after the ceiling was finished, the paintings were added, with the whole being completed in 1595. The central panel, set within a carved and gilded surround, is the *Triumph of Venice*, painted by Jacopo and Domenico Tintoretto.

Also noteworthy are the *Dead Christ Supported by Angels and worshipped by Doges Pietro Lando and Marcantonio Trevisan with their Patron Saints*, by Tintoretto and assistants (on the wall above the dais) and, on the opposite wall, the *Doges Lorenzo and Gerolamo Priuli Praying to the Virgin* by Palma il Giovane. On the wall opposite the windows are two large clocks, one of which bears the Signs of the Zodiac.

Sala del Consiglio dei Dieci

The Consiglio dei Dieci [Council of Ten] was a magistracy created in 1310 to deal with the Tiepolo-Querini conspiracy. It retained its emergency character for a long time, until in 1455 a decree of the Maggior Consiglio [Great Council] made it permanent. Empowered to investigate anyone who might threaten the security of the State, its meetings were shrouded in mystery.

As its name implies, it consisted of ten ordinary members, apart from the doge himself; these were chosen by the Senate and elected by the Maggior Consiglio.

The Sala del Consiglio dei Dieci was restructured in 1533-1550 by Scarpagnino, and work at once began on the paintings – by Ponchino, a young Veronese and Zelotti. The twenty-five panels of the ceiling were the first to be completed (1553-1554); the iconographical scheme was probably devised by Daniele Barbaro and consists largely of allegorical representations of the various

Paolo Caliari, known as Veronese, Aged Oriental Man and Young Woman, 1553-1555. Sala del Consiglio dei Dieci, ceiling.

Paolo Caliari, known as Veronese, Juno offering Venice with the Ducal Corno, 1553-1555. Sala del Consiglio dei Dieci, ceiling. The corno was the characteristic hat worn by the doge.

functions of the councillors who met in this chamber (the central panel is, however, a nineteenth-century copy of the original work by Veronese, now in the Louvre). Among the finest paintings in this room are: An *Aged Oriental Man and a Young Woman* and *Juno Offering the Ducal Corno to Venice*, by Paolo Veronese, while on the wall opposite the windows there is an *Adoration of the Magi* by Aliense. The painting of *Pope Alexander III Blessing Doge Ziani* was begun by Francesco Bassano but completed by assistants. The furnishings are at least in part original, but the seats of the members of the Council have been destroyed.

The Sala della Bussola

This is the first room on this floor dedicated to the administration of justice; its name comes from the large wooden compass (*bussola*) surmounted by a statue of Justice which stands in one corner and hides the entrance to the Sala dei Tre Capi del Consiglio dei Dieci e degli Inquisitori (which can only be visited as part of the Secret Itineraries tour). This room was the antechamber where those summoned before "The Ten" waited to be called; and the magnificent decor was intended to underline the solemnity of the Republic's legal machinery, some of the most famous and relentless exponents of which operated in these rooms. The decor dates from the sixteenth century, and once again it was Paolo Veronese who was commissioned to decorate the ceiling. Completed in 1554, the works he produced are all intended to exalt the "good government" of the Venetian Republic; the central panel, with *St. Mark Descending to crown the three Theological Virtues*, is a copy of the original, now in the Louvre. The large fireplace was designed by Jacopo Sansovino in 1553-54.

Within the palace, all the rooms which served in the exercise of justice were linked vertically. From the ground-floor prisons known as Pozzi [Wells], to the Avogaria [Advocates' Offices] on the loggia floor, the Quarantie [Tribunals of Forty] and the Sala del Magistrato alle Leggi [Hall of the Magistrates of Law]on the first floor and the various courtrooms on this second floor, the progression culminated in the prisons directly under the roof, the famous Piombi [Leads]. All of these spaces were interconnected by stairways, corridors and vestibules.From this room, in fact, one can pass to the Armoury and the Prigioni Nuove [New Prisons], on the other side of the Ponte dei Sospiri [Bridge of Sighs], or else go straight down the Scala dei Censori to pass into the rooms housing the councils of justice on the first floor.

HENRICI IV FRANCIÆ ET NAVARÆ REGIS ARMA
IN TOT, TANTISQ, ET PERICVLIS, ET VICTORIIS HOSTILI
SANGVINE MADEFACTA IMMORTALIS EIVS GLORIÆ TROPHÆVM
AC VERI, ET SINCERI AMORIS ERGA REMPVB.
MONVMENTVM

Armour which belonged to Henri IV of France. Armoury, Room II.

The various rooms of the Armoury contain a valuable historical collection of weapons and armaments from various sources. The core of the collection is already documented as existing in the fourteenth century; and at the time of the Republic the Armoury, under the control of the Consiglio dei Dieci [Council of Ten], was stocked with weapons that would be readily available for the palace guards. On particularly delicate or important occasions, these guards might be joined by the *arsenalotti*, the highly-trained workforce from the shipyards of the Arsenale. For example, when a doge died, all the gates to the Palace were sealed and placed under the guard of the *arsenalotti* (a group of whom was also usually present guarding the loggetta of the bell-tower when the Maggior Consiglio was in session).Comprising various valuable pieces, the collection of arms was partially dispersed after the fall of the Republic, but it still contains more than two thousand exhibits.

These include very famous examples of fifteenth- and sixteenth-century suits of armour, along with swords, halberds, quivers and crossbows. These often bear the inscribed or painted monogram CX – for Condìsiglio dei Dieci – which also appears on the door jambs; further evidence of the might of the Council.

Room I

This is named after Erasmo da Narni, the great condottiere better known as Gattamelata; in the large display case to the right as you enter is a suit of armour traditionally claimed to have belonged to him. Note the characteristic motif of the head of a cat [*gatto*] between two profiles of wolves' heads on the breastplate, the knee armour and the saddle. The same display case also contains the Duodo suit of armour (first on the left) and armour for a child (or dwarf?) recovered from the battlefield of Marignano (1515). In the case to the left of the door leading through to Room II are two small "tournament" suits of armour dating from 1490; the more lightweight brigandine alongside was used above all in foot combat. The other showcases in this room contain swords from various periods, as well as morions and crossbows (with their characteristic quivers in painted or embossed leather). Alongside there are also some lamps taken from enemy Turkish ships; note the half-moon crowning them.

Room II

The triangular Turkish standard hanging from the ceiling was seized from the Ottoman fleet during the battle of Lepanto in 1571. The borders are embroidered with verses from the Koran, and the central inscription is a declaration of homage to Allah and his prophet Mohammed. On the right, at the far end of the room, is armour which the French King Henri IV presented to the Republic in 1604; also on the right is a fifteenth-century example of an armoured headpiece for a horse. The large two-handed swords in the central display case were used in single combat. The room also contains two musket halberds.

Room III

The room is named after Francesco Morosini, whose bust can be seen in the niche in the far wall. Appointed Supreme Commander of the Venetian Fleet, this admiral would in the 1684-1688 war against the Turks re-conquer the Peloponnese; hence his nickname of "the Peloponnesian." Elected doge in 1688, his numerous victories would lead to him being the only Venetian ever to be honoured with a monument during his lifetime. The Museo Correr – one of the other museums in the St. Mark's area – contains more material relating to this extraordinary figure.

Room IV

This contains a surprising collection of various weapons: crossbows, maces, battle-axes, and so-called "musket swords" (these sixteenth-century weapons combined blade and firepower). In the display case against the end wall are various instruments of torture and

Armoury, View of Room 3, the Morosini Room.

weapons that were forbidden because too small (and therefore easily hidden about the person). The collection once belonged to the Carrara family of Padua, who were defeated by the Venetians in 1405. Note, in particular, the trick pieces – apparently innocuous objects, such as a box or a key, that contained deadly weapons. The room also contains a series of seventeenth-century harquebuses presented to doge Marino Grimani by a Persian ambassador in 1602; the various instruments of torture include a chastity belt. From the Armoury you now return to the first floor, to visit the rooms occupied by the organs of Venetian government. From there you pass on to the prisons.

The Liagò

From the Armoury, the intinerary of the visit brings you on to this room and then the others on the second floor.

In Venetian dialect a *liagò* is a terrace or veranda enclosed by glass. This particular example was a sort of corridor and meeting-place for patrician members of the Maggior Consiglio in the intervals between their discussions of government business.

The ceiling of painted and gilded beams dates from the middle of the sixteenth century, whilst the paintings on the walls are seventeenth- and eighteenth-century. The gallery also contains three important works of sculpture: *Adam, Eve* and *The Shield-Bearer*. These are the originals produced to adorn the façades of the Foscari Porch in the courtyard of the Palace. The work of Antonio Rizzo,

View of the Liagò.

Antonio Rizzo, Adam and Eve, *fifteenth century. Liagò.*

they were sculpted between 1462 and 1471 and are masterpieces of realistic modelling and psychological insight.

The Sala della Quarantia Civil Vecchia

Here the itinerary continues with a visit to the rooms in which justice was administered.

The Quarantia [Tribunal of Forty] seems to have been set up by the Maggior Consiglio [Great Council] at the end of the twelfth century and was the highest appeal court in the Republic. Originally a single forty-man tribunal which wielded substantial political and legislative power, the Quarantia was during the course of the fifteenth century divided into three separate Councils: the Quarantia Criminal (for sentences in what we would call criminal law); the Quarantia Civil Vecchia (for civil actions within Venice) and the Quarantia Civil

View of the Sala della Quarantia Civil Vecchia.

Pietro Malombra, God the Father, Venice Enthroned, the Virtues and Mercury leading the old and the young in chains, c. 1615 (detail). Sala della Quarantia Civil Vecchia.

Nuova (for civil actions within the Republic's mainland territories). The Sala della Quarantia Civil Vecchia was the meeting-place for the forty members of the Quarantia Civile. The room's present appearance is due to a series of alterations in the course of the seventeenth century.

On the walls are paintings by Pietro Malombra, *God the Father, Venice Enthroned with the Virtues and Mercury Leading the Old and the Young in Chains*.

The room also contains: a tabernacle with a fifteenth-century panel of the *Madonna and Child*; two canvases by Andrea Celesti depicting *Moses Destroying the Golden Calf* and *Moses Chastising the Jews for their Idolatry*; and Giovan Battista Lorenzetti's *Venice among the Virtues Receiving the Sceptre of Power* (1660). An ancient fragment of painting in which the upper part of St. Mark's Basilica is still visible has been found under the wooden dossals.

Sala dell'Armamento

The Sala dell'Armamento (also known as the Sala del Guariento) was a storeroom for weapons and munitions, and was originally connected to the Sala d'Armi and the Sala del Consiglio dei Dieci on the upper floors. At present it contains the remains of a fresco by Guariento, formerly in the Sala del Maggior Consiglio.

Commissioned in about 1365, this represents the *Coronation of the Virgin*. Badly damaged in the fire of 1577, it was then concealed behind the canvas of Tintoretto's *Paradise*; almost forgotten thereafter, it was only brought to light in the early years of the twentieth century.

Sala del Maggior Consiglio

The Sala del Maggior Consiglio was the chamber where the most important legislative body of the Venetian State gathered to deliberate. The Maggior Consiglio was a very ancient body, comprising all noble Venetians above twenty years of age, whose mandate lasted one year (but they could stand for re-election). The assemblies were always presided over by the doge and the Signoria. In 1297 the *Serrata* (or closure) of the Maggior Consiglio restricted those eligible for membership, making a seat on the Council practically permanent. Up to that time, the whole administration of the Venetian state had effectively been in the hands of the Maggior Consiglio; and even after that date, when legislative power had passed to the Senate, the Council still retained certain important prerogatives, such as the power to grant pardons. Its meetings were secret until the sixteenth century. The chamber was built in the mid-fourteenth century, and the earliest paintings date from 1365. In that year Guariento, a Paduan artist, was commissioned to paint a fresco of the *Coronation of the Virgin* on the wall behind the throne. This fresco was then badly damaged during the fire of 1577; what remains of it can now be seen in the Sala del Guariento.

The great fire of 1577 damaged both the wooden fittings and the

architecture of the Sala del Maggior Consiglio, whilst canvases and frescoes by such important artists as Gentile da Fabriano, Antonio Veneziano, Michelino da Besozzo, Alvise Vivarini, Jacobello del Fiore and Michele Giambono were almost completely destroyed.

So extensive was the damage that the Signoria at first considered completely rebuilding the chamber. Finally, partial reconstruction – to a design by Antonio Rusconi – was decided upon; this retained the surviving features of the original, and the result is what one can see today. First, it was decided to decorate the ceiling (by Cristoforo Sorte, 1582), and in 1587 a monk, Gerolamo dei Bardi,

Jacopo Robusti, known as Tintoretto, Doge Nicolò da Ponte receives a Laurel Crown from Venice, *1584. Sala del Maggior Consiglio.*

Jacopo Palma il Giovane, The Crusader Army Attacks Constantinople, *c. 1587. Sala del Maggior Consiglio.*

Paolo Caliari, known as Veronese, The Thriumph of Venice, *1582. Sala del Maggior Consiglio.*

Jacopo Palma il Giovane, Crowned by Victory, Venice Receives her Subject Provinces, *1582-1584. Sala del Maggior Consiglio.*

Jacopo Robusti, known as Tintoretto, The Venetian Victory over Ferrara at Argenta, *1579-1584. Sala del Maggior Consiglio, ceiling.*

Domenico Tintoretto, Portraits of Doges Giovanni Mocenigo and Mario Barbarigo, *1580-1590. Sala del Maggior Consiglio.*

was commissioned to draft a detailed iconographic scheme which brought together episodes from the history of relations between pope and emperor, incidents from the Fourth Crusade and other symbolic themes more strictly celebratory of Venice.

The central space was reserved for the glorification of the Republic. The design of the ceiling was conceived, in the taste of the period, as a sequence of large panels in which paintings on canvas were enclosed within sumptuous carved and gilded frames. There are three great paintings in the centre and twelve at the sides, while

the spaces between the frames are filled with monochrome depictions of historical episodes or allegorical subjects. This imposing complex of decoration was completed in the years of doge Nicolò da Ponte, and as usual the most celebrated painters of the day were commissioned for the task. In 1579 Tintoretto and Veronese began work, followed by Jacopo Palma il Giovane and Francesco Bassano. The ceiling was completed by 1584, while the walls, begun in about 1590, were probably only completed early in the seventeenth century. The one exception is Tintoretto's enormous painting of *Paradise*, on which the artist worked from 1588 to 1594. Veronese's *Triumph of Venice*, a particularly rich and spectacular work, is set in the ceiling above the throne, with the central space in the room being occupied by the 1584 painting *Nicolò da Ponte Receiving the Laurel Crown from Venice*, by Tintoretto (though probably some of the the the work is his assistants'). On the end wall is Jacopo Palma il Giovane's *Crowned by Victory, Venice Receives Her Subject Provinces*; many preparatory studies for this work are still extant. The twelve paintings at the sides of the ceiling (six per side) represent acts of heroism by the Republic's condottieri or other episodes of war. They include: *The Venetian Victory over the Milanese under Filippo Maria Visconti*, by Palma il Giovane; *Contarini's Conquest*

Paola Caliari known as Veronese, Doge Contarini Returning to Venice in Triumph after Defeating the Genoese, 1585-1586. Sala del Maggior Consiglio.

Jacopo Robusti, known as Tintoretto, Paradise, 1588-1594. Sala del Maggior Consiglio.

of *Riva del Garda* by Tintoretto and assistants; and *The Battle of Maclodio* by Francesco Bassano. Immediately below the ceiling there runs a frieze with portraits of the first seventy-six doges, from Obelerio Antenoreo to Francesco Venier (1554-1556). The commission for these portraits – most of which are purely imaginary – was given to Jacopo Tintoretto, but they are mainly the work of his son Domenico. Each doge holds a scroll on which are illustrated the most important achievements of his reign. A typical instance of *damnatio memoriae* can be seen in the frieze of the Doges of Venice: doge Marin Faliero (1354-1355) was beheaded for conspiracy against the state, and in the panel where his portrait should appear there is a black curtain with this inscription: HIC EST LOCUS MARINI FALETHRI DECAPITATI PRO CRIMINIBUS (this is the place of Marin Faliero, beheaded for his crimes). Of all the paintings on the walls, the most impressive is probably Tintoretto's *Paradise*, commissioned in 1588. A vast canvas – in which Tintoretto was assisted by his son, Domenico – this richly imaginative composition is made up of a huge number of figures, each endowed with a powerful sense of movement. Painted in sections at the Scuola Vecchia della Misericordia, this massive work was then "assembled"

here and the final details added. The works on the wall towards the inner courtyard were painted later, in the late sixteenth and early seventeenth centuries, and – as mentioned above – depict Venice's mediation between Papacy and Empire. Amongst the episodes is a depiction of the origin of the symbols of authority carried by doges in public processions (though, in fact, these dated back to Byzantine times and were not, as is suggested here, the result of papal grant).

The sequence of the twelve episodes starts with Carlo and Gabriele Caliari's *Alexander III in Venice with Doge Ziani*, near the dais. The other historical cycle, running along the wall on the waterfront side of the room, depicts episodes from the Fourth Crusade, which was of great importance for Venice's subsequent commercial expansion in the East. Among the canvases of this cycle are *The Crusader Army Besieges Zara* by Andrea Vicentino; the *Surrender of Zara* and *The Conquest of Constantinople* by Domenico Tintoretto; and *The Crusaders Besieging Constantinople* by Jacopo Palma il Giovane. On the wall opposite the dais, in the centre, is *Doge Contarini Returning to Venice in Triumph after Defeating the Genoese*, by Paolo Veronese and assistants, commemorating the victory of 1379.

The Maggior Consiglio

Paolo Caliari, known
as Veronese, Pietro Mocenigo
Commanding the Attack
on the City of Smyrna, 1580.
Sala del Maggior Consiglio,
ceiling.

The meetings of the Maggior Consiglio were normally held on
Sundays, and were preceded by the ringing of the bell of St. Mark's.
The Signoria and the Concilio dei Dieci [Council of Ten] were
responsible for ensuring that meetings were held behind closed
doors and no weapons were brought into the chamber. The
members, except for certain office-holders, would be seated in two
rows, back-to-back. During the assemblies, armed guards were
drawn up on both the Ponte della Paglia and in the Piazza, under
the charge of the Procurators of St. Mark, who waited under the
loggia of the bell tower. It was in this chamber that the preliminary
stages of the election of the doge took place; voting would then
be continued in the Sala dello Scrutinio.

The election of a doge was a particularly long and complicated
procedure, in which voting alternated with the drawing of lots.
A number of ballots, corresponding to the number of nobles
present, were placed in an urn; thirty of them were marked with
the word *lector*. Whoever received a ballot so marked remained
in the chamber, the others left the room. The same procedure
was repeated to choose the electors, who in turn nominated forty
new *lectores*; then, by drawing lots, these were reduced to twelve,
who elected twenty-five people and they, with a further ballot,
were reduced to five. These in turn had to elect forty-three people,
reduced to eleven again by drawing lots. These eleven elected
the forty-one electors of the doge, who required a minimum
of twenty-five votes to be elected.

The Venetian Constitution

Like all the states of the *Ancien Régime*, Venice had no codified, written
constitution. Its political system had evolved from that of a *commune* –
a city-state structure that was typical of the Italian Middle Ages
and saw power entrusted to an oligarchy (in Venice's case, a patrician
merchant class) whose interests were identified with those of the
population as a whole. The thing that distinguishes Venice is that –
faced with such mighty European powers as Spain, France, the Holy
Roman Empire and the Papacy – it was still able to withstand the,
elsewhere irresistible, aggression of Absolute Monarchy. In effect,
it preserved its, by then archaic, system right up until the eve of the
nineteenth century. Once the hegemony of the patrician class was
firmly in place – from the end of the thirteenth century onwards –
a constitutional mechanism was set in place to prevent any family or
faction overwhelming the other members of the oligarchy. Elsewhere in
Italy there were far too many examples of ruling dynasties which had
come to power thanks to internecine strife within governing oligarchies,
and Venice was determined that the patrician management of power
should remain collegial. The Maggior Consiglio was limited to the
adult males of those families inscribed within the "Golden Book,"
a sort of birth register of the patrician class. The sovereign body of the
State, this Council then elected all the major governing councils of the
Republic: the Senato, the Quarantie [Tribunals of Forty], the Signoria
and the Dieci. These committees had legislative, executive and judicial
powers that were vast and yet rather imperfectly defined.
What was rigorously defined was the length of time an individual
could hold office: never more than a few months. This constant
turn-over obviously left its mark on the public career of any ambitious
nobleman; but it also served to guarantee that his colleagues could
keep an ever-watchful eye on his activities. The possession of an
overseas and Italian "empire" – the *territorio da Mare* and the *territorio
da Terra* respectively – made the Republic a mighty power both in the
Mediterranean and on the European stage. Nevertheless, Venice
remained above all a city-state. Undoubtedly a great metropolis – then
amongst the most densely-populated in the world – it cared little about
the social or political equilibrium within the cities and lands under
its dominion. Its primary concern was internal peace, defence, correct
payment of taxes and respect for all those privileges reserved to those
who were citizens of the proud *Dominante*.

The Sala dello Scrutinio

From this room one enters the fifteenth-century wing of the Palace. It was here that the precious codices which Petrarch and Cardinal Bessarione had left to the Republic were housed before the building of the Biblioteca Marciana. Thereafter, in 1532, it was decided to use this chamber for the voting procedures, hence its present name. The decor dates between 1578 and 1615. The richly-decorated ceiling was designed by the painter-cartographer Cristoforo Sorte and the thirty-nine panels within it depict the conquest of Padua in 1405 and Venetian naval victories in the East; the layout of the subject-matter was according to a scheme drawn up

View of the Sala dello Scrutinio.

Morosini Doorway, Sala dello Scrutinio.

Francesco Da Ponte, known as Bassano, The Conquest of Padua at Night, *1583-1584. Sala dello Scrutinio.*

by the monk Gerolamo dei Bardi. Almost all the works were commissioned from Tintoretto, Veronese and their pupils; however, there were alterations to the original plan, and some of the present paintings date from the following century. The frieze continues the sequence of portraits of doges which we have already seen in the Sala del Maggior Consiglio. The first portraits are the work of Tintoretto and his assistants; the others, which continue right up to Doge Ludovico Manin (1789-1797) were by artists who were contemporaries of their subjects. On the wall occupied by the tribunal there is the beautiful *Last Judgement* by Palma il Giovane (1594-1595, complete with the coat-of-arms of Doge Francesco Foscari); this replaced a work on the same

Pietro Liberi, The Venetian Victory over the Turks in the Dardanelles, *1660-1665. Sala dello Scrutinio.*

subject by Tintoretto, which had been irreparably damaged in a fire. On the end wall, towards the Scala Foscara, there is the monument to Francesco Morosini (c. 1694); designed by Gaspari, this contains paintings of the admiral's military achievements by Lazzarini. From the Sala dello Scrutinio, the itinerary brings you back through the Sala del Maggior Consiglio and, by a little door to the right of the doge's throne, into a corridor from which you turn almost immediately right into the Sala della Quarantia Criminal.

The Sala della Quarantia Criminal and the Sala dei Cuoi

Housing one of the three Quarantie [Tribunals of Forty, *quaranta* = forty], the highest appeal courts in the Venetian Republic, this is another room used in the administration of justice.

The Quarantia Criminal was set up in the fifteenth century and, as the name suggests, dealt with cases of criminal law. It was a very important body as its members, who were part of the Senate as well, also had legislative powers.

The wooden stalls date from the seventeenth century. The room beyond this served as an archive, and was presumably lined with shelves and cupboards, similar to that one can now see on the far

wall. This was not part of the original furnishings, nor were the
cuoridoro, the gold-embossed panelling one can see on the
other walls.

The Sala del Magistrato alle Leggi

This chamber housed the Magistratura dei conservatori ed esecutori
delle leggi e ordini degli uffici di San Marco e di Rialto, to give them
their full title. Created in 1553, this authority was headed by three
of the city's patricians and was responsible for making sure the
regulations concerning the practice of law were observed.
In a mercantile city such as Venice, the courts were of enormous
importance; and the administration of justice in the city was made

Hieronymus Bosch, Diptych with Scenes of Heaven, *1500-1504, left panel. Sala del Magistrato alle Leggi.*

Hieronymus Bosch, Diptych with Scenes of Heaven, *1500-1504, right panel. Sala del Magistrato alle Leggi.*

Quentin Metsys, The Mocking of Christ, *early sixteenth century. Sala del Magistrato alle Leggi.*

all the more exceptional by the fact that it was not based on Imperial, Common or Roman Law but on a legal system that was peculiar to Venice.

This Chamber now houses the extraordinary Hieronymus Bosch triptych which Cardinal Domenic Grimani left to the Republic in 1523 – a work that for many years hung in the Chamber of the Three Heads of the Consiglio dei Dieci (which today can only be visited as part of the Secret Itineraries tour).

The pictures have all the characteristic features of Bosch's painting: painstaking rendition of details and landscapes; delight in anecdote; disturbing and mysterious symbols; and that playful satirical tone with which the artist denounces the folly of humanity and the demonic influence at work in human affairs.

Dealing with such themes as temptation, sin, redemption, punishment and human vices, Bosch's work is one of the greatest expressions of the obsessive moral concerns behind that new mysticism which emerged as the Renaissance first began to make itself felt in the mediaeval world of Northern Europe.

The itinerary now takes you to the Prigioni Nuove [New Prisons], access to which is via the Ponte dei Sospiri [Bridge of Sighs].

The Ponte dei Sospiri

Leaving the Sala del Magistrato alle Leggi, a small staircase takes you down to a narrow stone-clad corridor. This is one of the two passageways across the famous Ponte dei Sospiri, which was initially designed by Rusconi, continued by Da Ponte and completed by Antonio and Tommaso Contin (1614). Intended to link the palace with the building of the Prigioni Nuove on the other side of the canal, this enclosed structure is richly decorated in a taste that

Antonio Rusconi, Antonio Da Ponte, Antonio and Tommaso Contin, The Ponte dei Sospiri, seventeenth century.

The two passageways within the Ponte dei Sospiri, seen from the entrance on the Prigioni Nuove side.

The Prigioni Nuove, courtyard.

seems to herald the innovations of the Baroque; there is also a bas-relief of Justice and the coat-of-arms of doge Marino Grimani (1595-1605). The name of the bridge, however, is a more modern romantic invention and dates from the nineteenth century. Designed by Da Ponte but actually completed by Antonio Contin at the beginning of the seventeenth century, the Prigioni Nuove [New Prisons] replaced the gaol within the Palace itself, which by the end of the sixteenth century was too small to hold the number of prisoners awaiting trial or serving their sentence. The bridge linking the two structures was designed to facilitate transport from cell to courtroom – and before the nineteenth century its associations were far from romantic.

The Prigioni Nuove

Reached by the Ponte dei Sospiri, this prison block was built to designs which were in part the work of a man already serving a life sentence; and, in fact, what is striking about them is the attention paid to the living conditions of the around three hundred prisoners the building was intended to hold: the cells were bigger and had more light and air. In short, they were designed to be more humane.

This solicitude for the prisoner's lot was rather rare at the time, and made a further contribution to the severe but paternalistic image of its justice system which the Republic tried to nurture.

Visitors today can choose a short or longer tour of the prisons. The former takes you quickly through the building and almost immediately back onto the Ponte dei Sospiri and into the Doge's Palace once more. The longer tour includes a greater number of cells, the prison courtyard – from which it is possible to appreciate the mass of this stone structure – and a room which contains wall segments with graffiti left by recent prisoners held

Corridor and cells in the Prigioni Nuove.

Cell with wood panelling, Prigioni Nuove.

in the building (which continued to be used as a gaol right up to the 1930s). There is also an interesting collection of the ceramics recovered during excavation work in the city and the lagoon; recent research has revealed these to be an invaluable source of information regarding the origins of Venetian culture.

Ceramics Recovered from Archaeological Excavations.

The display cases contain artisan objects – primarily in ceramics – which date from the Roman period right up to the modern day. Recovered by the Superintendence for Venice's Environmental and Architectural Heritage during excavations prior to restoration work, these have been studied using the most advanced scientific techniques.

The oldest pieces are fragments of amphoras dating from the Roman period, Late Antiquity and the Early Middle Ages. Together with food remains (animal bones and mollusc shells), they were unearthed at the deepest layers of the excavation in St. Mark's Square which followed the collapse of the bell-tower in 1902; other more recent pieces, dating from the sixteenth and seventeenth century, were found in the upper layers.

Excavation work at the church of San Lorenzo di Castello brought to light various locally-produced ceramic works dating from the ninth-tenth century, together with vases of Byzantine or Middle-Eastern manufacture dating from the eleventh-twelfth century. A lot of the ceramics material – bowls, pots, plates and jugs – is adorned with inscribed decoration. Most of the material, dating from the fourteenth to sixteenth century, comes from the excavation work at Malamocco and at the site of the Venice State Archives (in the former monastery of the Frari). Along with numerous locally-produced pieces, this contains various fragments of imported work (particularly that of Spanish-Moorish origin). More recent excavations at the Doge's Palace, the Prigioni Nuove and the State Archives have revealed the great continuity in local ceramic production, right up until the early years of the nineteenth century. The itinerary of the visit now takes you back across the Ponte dei Sospiri to the Sala dei Censori in the Doge's Palace.

The Sala dei Censori

The State Censors were set up in 1517 by Marco Foscari di Giovanni, a cousin of doge Andrea Gritti (1523-1538) and nephew of the great Francesco Foscari.

View of the Sala dei Censori.
View of the Sala dell'Avogaria de Comun.

The title and duties of the Censors resulted from the cultural and political upheavals that are associated with Humanism. In fact, the Censors were not judges as such, but more like moral consultants – a role that is clear from the fact that they were only two in number, and thus incapable of giving a majority ruling. Their main task was the repression of electoral fraud and the protection of the State's public institutions. On the walls hang a number of Domenico Tintoretto's portraits of these magistrates, and below the armorial bearings of some of those who held the post.

The Sala dell'Avogaria de Comun

This room was occupied by the Avogaria de Comun, a magistracy first founded in the twelfth century. Elected by the Maggior Consiglio [Great Council], the three *avogadori* who made up this body were responsible for overseeing the correct application of Venetian law. Though these three never achieved the prestige or power of the Consiglio dei Dieci [Council of Ten], they did remain one of the most authoritative state bodies within the Republic right up until its fall in 1797. They were also responsible for guaranteeing the purity of the

Leandro da Ponte, known as Bassano, Madonna in Glory with three Avogadori, *c. 1604. Sala dell'Avogaria.*

Domenico Tintoretto, Resurrection with three Avogadori, *c. 1576. Sala dell'Avogaria.*

Venetian aristocracy as a caste – that is, overseeing the legitimacy of marriages and births within the families of those nobleman who were inscribed in the Golden Book. The portraits of *avogadori* on the walls include works by Jacopo and Domenico Tintoretto.

The Sala dello Scrigno

The Venetian nobility as a caste came into existence because of the "closure" of admissions to the Maggior Consiglio in 1297; however, it was only in the sixteenth century that formal measures were taken to introduce restrictions that protected the status of that aristocracy: marriages between noblefolk and commoners were forbidden, and greater controls were set up to check the validity of aristocratic titles, etc. The enforcement of these restrictions came within the duties of the Avogaria Comun, also responsible for drawing up the "Golden Book," within which were registered the baptismal vows of each new-born patrician (if a baptism was not so registered, the aristocrat concerned risked finding himself excluded from the Maggior Consiglio and thus from any role in the city's political life). It later became compulsory for each aristocrat to produce a marriage certificate before the Avogaria, irrespective of the social status of his wife. There was also a "Silver Book." This registered all those families which, whilst not aristocratic, could demonstrate requisites of "civilisation" and "honour" as well as the fact that they were

View of the Sala dello Scrigno.

View of the Sala della Milizia da Mar.

of ancient Venetian origin. It was these which furnished the manpower for the State bureaucracy – and, in particular, the chancellery within the Doge's Palace itself.

The "Golden" and "Silver Books" were kept in a chest [*scrigno*] in this room, inside a cupboard that also contained all the documents proving the legitimacy of claims to be inscribed therein.

The cabinet which one sees here nowadays extends around three sides of a wall niche; lacquered in white with gilded decorations, it dates from the eighteenth century.

The Sala della Milizia da Mar

Made up of twenty members of the Senate and the Maggior Consiglio, the Milizia da Mar [Naval Office] was a body first set up in the middle of the sixteenth century and was responsible for recruiting the crews necessary for Venice's war galleys. This was no easy task, given the large number of people required by the city's extensive fleet. Contrary to what one might expect, the bulk of these crews were made up of paid oarsman drawn from the Venetian manufacturing industries – that is, from those various crafts and guilds which had a direct interest in preserving the city.

Another similar body, entitled the Provveditori all'armar, was responsible for the actual fitting and supplying of the fleet.
The furnishings and covered furniture are sixteenth-century, whilst the wall torches date from the eighteenth century.

End of the Itinerary

The following room used to house the Lower Chancellery of the Doge's Palace and now contains a bookshop; from here, one can go down to the cafeteria on the lower floor which occupies the atmospheric setting of what were the palace kitchens. Otherwise, you can go out into the loggia directly opposite the head of the Scala dei Giganti, which forms a single axis with the Foscari entrance and the Porta della Carta; note the copies of the two statues of *Adam* and *Eve* which Antonio Rizzo carved for the Foscari Arch (the originals are now in the Liagò). In the wall opposite the head of the Staircase is a plaque commemorating the visit to Venice by Henri III of France in 1574. to the right of the Scala dei Giganti is the Scala dei Senatori , which leads down to the courtyard of the same name. From here one passes through the Foscari Entrance to leave the palace by the Gothic Porta della Carta.

THE SECRET ITINERARY

Giovan Battista Zelotti, Time, the Virtues and Envy Liberated from Evil (detail). Sala dei Tre Capi, ceiling.

The Secret Itinerary through the Doge's Palace covers the rooms and chambers where the work of some of the most important bodies in the Venetian administration was carried out. The tour offers an interesting insight into the civil and political history of the city, its public organisations and the administration of justice. The visit must be pre-booked, and can only take place – times and conditions to be requested at the Museum Information Desk – in the company of a special guide who will explain all the special features of each individual room. The itinerary starts at a small wooden door in the wall of the Atrio Quadrato opposite the Sala delle Quattro Porte. From here you enter several small interconnected rooms, the space for which was in part created by the installation of false ceilings. On this floor there are the rooms of the **Notaio Ducale** and the **Deputato alla Segreta**, above which are those of the **Cancellier Grande** and **Segretario alle Voci**;

These were all functionaries with delicate administrative tasks.

View of the Sala dei Tre Capi.

Next comes the **Sala dei Tre Capi**, the magistracy that reported to

Office of the Cancellier Grande.

The Sala della Cancelleria Superiore, responsible for State Archives.

the Consiglio dei Dieci; this is decorated with paintings by Veronese and Ponchino, whilst the following **Sala degli Inquisitori** is decorated by Tintoretto. The precise title of this much-feared magistracy was "Inquisitors for the Protection of State Secrets;" set up in 1539, it dealt – in absolute secrecy – with delicate questions of State security. A flight of stairs leads to the top floor, where there

is the vast **Sala della Cancelleria Segreta**, which is lined with solid walls of cabinets. The upper mirrors on each cabinet door are decorated with the coat-of-arms of the various Chancellors from 1268 onwards. After the **Sala della Cancelleria**, you pass through the **Sala del Reggente** and the **Sala del Vice-Reggente** to the rather disturbing **Sala della Tortura**, whose name needs no explanation. From here, a series of narrow passageways leads to the **area of the Piombi prisons,** which can also be reached from the Sala dei Tre Capi. The various cells of the Piombi – the name derives from the lead-sheeting on the roof above – were occupied by the prisoners of the Consiglio dei Dieci or the State Inquisitors (generally those awaiting trial or convicted of non-serious crimes). The six or seven cells are subdivided into three blocks: the first is exactly above the Sala dei Tre Capi, the other two are on the canalside of the wing.

The Piombi cells include the ones made famous by the vivid description Casanova gives of his imprisonment and escape.

After the fall of the Republic – when the Doge's Palace became the seat for the administration of justice with the Austrian-ruled Veneto – the Piombi continued to be used as cells. At the beginning of the Italian Risorgimento they were used to hold the writer Silvio Pellico, who was awaitng trail for sedition; his subsequent account of his ten years in the terrible Moravian prison of Spielberg (*Le mie prigioni*) would ultimately "cost Austria more dearly than any defeat on the battlefield."

Casanova's Imprisonment

The escape from the cells of the Piombi is perhaps the most famous incident in Casanova's life; and undoubtedly his being there in the first place serves to illustrate the tense relationship which existed between the renowned "rake" and the government of the Serenissima. At the time of Casanova, the administration of justice in Venice was divided between various bodies and tribunals: the Quarantia Criminal – a "high court" for serious crimes, this followed procedures that offered some protection of the accused's rights; the Consiglio dei Dieci, responsible for State security and therefore much more secretive, summary and inquisitorial in its handling of the accused; and the State Inquisitors proper, who worked in collaboration with the Consiglio dei Dieci but were even less mindful of "civil rights." Alongside these main bodies there were others with very specific duties – for example, the Avogadori de Comun, the Signori di notte al criminal, the five Anziani alla Pace and even a body responsible for punishing blasphemy, the Esecutori contro la Bestemmia. One of the tasks of the State Inquisitors was intervention in situations that might undermine "the high image that

Portrait of Giacomo Casanova, in Jcosameron ou Histoire d'Edouard et diElisabeth..., *Prague s.a. [1787?].Venice, Biblioteca Nazionale Marciana.*

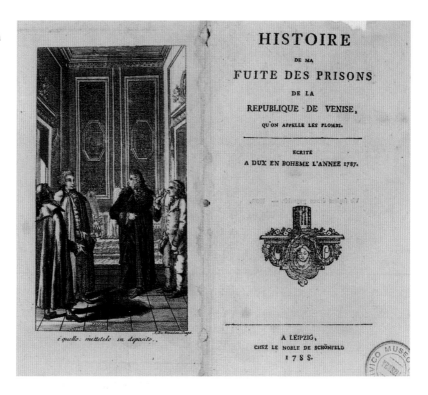

the Venetian patrician class should maintain of itself," and to this end they employed a network of informers, known as "confidantes." Though not a nobleman himself, Casanova would fall foul of this body in 1754, and there are numerous extant reports from those who had him under surveillance. The reason for his problems with the Inquisitors was only indirectly the result of his libertarian style of life, his gambling, his amorous adventures, his familiarity with forbidden books and the magic arts and his membership of the Freemasons. The real problem was his friendship with – and influence over – members of the patrician class, in particular Matteo Bragadin, Marco Dandolo, Marco Barbaro and the Memmo brothers. What is more, the fact that he frequented these people but also had contacts with foreigners in the city raised suspicions that Casanova might be engaged in espionage – hence the involvement of the State Inquisitors. On 26 July 1755 Casanova was arrested and taken to the Piombi, which – along with the Pozzi [wells] in the very depths of the Doge's Palace – were the two prisons used by the Inquisitors; those charged with crimes that involved other tribunals and investigating magistrates were held in the Prigioni Nuove on the other side of the Ponte dei Sospiri. As was the custom with such inquisitorial proceedings, Casanova was never told the charges against him or the sentence he had received.

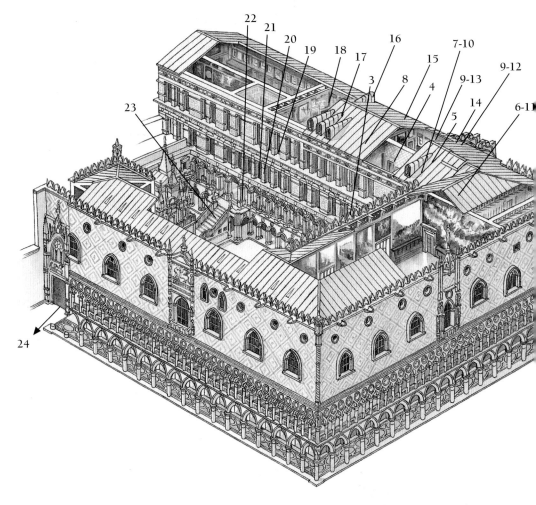

Imprisonment and Escape

Casanova gives a very compelling account of this experience in both
his *Memoirs* and the more specific *Histoire de ma Fuite des prisons de la
République de Venise qu'on appelle les Plombs*. In a gripping narrative,
he reveals great skill in drawing his characters and in analysing feelings
and emotions, producing a remarkable weave of truth and fabrication,
true anguish and irony. It is just such a combination of feelings that
is roused in the modern-day visitor to this place, where corridors and
stairways, walls and barred cells still carry an echo of its grim past.
What follows is a description of the gaol based on the account given
in Casanova's *Histoire de ma vie*; for despite the various "technical"
inexactitudes in his tale – and subsequent changes in the layout of the
Piombi – one can still use his autobiography as a sort of guidebook for
the imagination. Page references are to the Italian edition (eds. Piero
Chiara and Federico Roncoroni, vols I-III, Milan, 1983-1989). Now
part of the Secret Itineraries, the Piombi have been recently restored

to their layout and appearance in Casanova's day. The visit starts from the ground floor of the Prigioni Nuove (1). Passing through the entrance and across the courtyard, "we then climbed a number of steps which lead to a closed bridge [the Ponte dei Sospiri] that links the prisons with the Doge's Palace on the other side of the canal" (2). "Once over the bridge, we came [via various flights of stairs (3)] to a corridor that leads into one room and then another [these are the rooms of the Deputato alla Segreta and of the Notaio Ducale] (II, 5-6). It was here that Casanova's identity was formally certified by the Segretario degli Inquistori, and the prisoner was handed over to the gaoler responsible for the Piombi. After being taken through the Sala dei Tre Capi dei Dieci, this man then "led me up two narrow flights of stairs (5), along one corridor and then another and then another, at the end of which I found myself in a large loft space (6) feebly lit by a skylight high up in the roof. [Here] the gaoler took a large key, opened an iron-clad door that was three and a half feet tall, and told me to go inside." (II, 6). "Bewildered and in a state of collapse," Casanova had arrived in the infamous Piombi. The cells, six or seven in number, were divided into three groups (7), (8) and (9) and were located over three different rooms in the palace: the Sala degli Inquistori e dei Tre Capi, the Sala della Bussola and the upper landing of the Scala dei Censori. The first cell Casanova occupied was one of the three above the Sala degli Inquistori, overlooking the palace courtyard (10). The effect upon the prisoner was bound to have been terrible, not only because of the situation in which he found himself but also because he was told nothing about the reasons why he was there. At first, Casanova gave way to anger, then anguish. "I realised I had ended up in a place where the false seemed true and reality seemed some sort of bad dream; where the mind seems to lose its abilities and a deformed imagination can make one the victim of either chimerical hope or terrible desperation. I made a decision to keep all my wits about me, drawing upon all the philosophy I had in my soul but which I had never yet had occasion to use." (II, 10). Gradually the hopes of a quick release faded, and the prisoner's thoughts began to focus on a plan of escape. After nine months of imprisonment, Casanova was allowed to walk around the area under the roof for one half hour every day (11), and it was during one of these walks that he managed to get hold of the old iron doorbolt which became the tool around which he built his escape plan. With patience and tenacity, he set about digging a hole in the floor of his cell, with the intention of slipping down into the Sala degli Inquistori during the night and thence escaping from the palace. By the end of August, he had almost

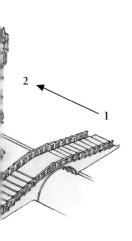

Section of the Doge's Palace with the route of Casanova's escape.

broken through, but then – totally unexpectedly – he was transferred to another cell, overlooking the canal and located above the upper landing of the Scala dei Censori (12). He managed to take the well-hidden bolt with him, but the hole in the previous cell was discovered, and it was only through a skilful application of psychology (and probably money) that Casanova managed to avoid it being reported the authorities. However, surveillance upon him was tightened. Casanova had by chance made contact with another prisoner, Marino Balbi, whose cell was part of the block above the Sala della Bussola (13); and on 29 September he was able to pass on the iron bolt to him. In just eight days Balbi had managed to scrape a hole in the ceiling of his cell (which he carefully hid behind religious images). Through this hole, the prisoner heaved himself up into the space directly under the roof and then worked on the wall that separated his cell from Casanova's. Having broken through on 16 October, he managed – after various vicissitudes – to create a hole in the ceiling of that cell, and thus the two could get up onto the roof itself. Scrambling along the

Giacomo Casanova escaping from the prisons of the Piombi, Histoire de ma fuite des prisons de Venise, *Leipzig 1788. Venice, Museo Correr.*

The Piombi, the corridor
leading towards the first cell
occupied by Casanova.

leaded roof, they found a skylight (16) and slipped back down into the
space beneath. There, Casanova says, "I found a narrow stone staircase
(17) and went down to another flight of stairs that ended at a glass
door. I opened that and finally found myself in a chamber that
I recognised (18)" (II, 121). However, the door was locked and it was
only with great difficulty that they managed to prise it open with the
iron bolt. Passing down a further two flights of stairs (19), they then
came to the Atrio Quadrato on the floor below (20). However, between
that and the Scala d'Oro was another heavy, locked door; nor was there
any way out of the other doors. By this time it was dawn; and when
Casanova looked out of a window he was seen by the night-watchman,
who mistook him for someone who had been inadvertently locked
in the second floor of the Palace overnight. Quick as a flash Casanova
and his accomplice hurried down that Staircase (21), turned right into
the loggia (22) and then left down the Scala dei Giganti, passing
through the arcade to the Porta della Carta and out of the Palace. He
would later write "I confess I am proud [of this escape]. But my pride
does not come from the fact that I managed to get away – because luck
played a large part in that – but from the fact that I considered the
whole undertaking possible and had the courage to attempt it."

Essential Bibliography

Michela Agazzi, *Platea Sancti Marci. I luoghi marciani dall'XI al XIII secolo e la formazione della piazza,* Venice, 1991.

Architettura e Utopia nella Venezia del Cinquecento, catalogue of the exhibition in the Doge's Palace, Milan 1980.

Elena Bassi, *Il Palazzo Ducale di Venezia,* 1971.

Elena Bassi, *Palazzi di Venezia. Admiranda Urbis Venetae,* Venice 1976.

Elena Bassi and Egle Renata Trincanato, *Il Palazzo Ducale nella Storia e nell'arte di Venezia,* Milan 1965.

Giorgio Bellavitis, *Venezia,* Rome 1980-1985.

Gino Benzoni, *I Dogi,* Milan 1982.

Giacomo Casanova, *Histoire de ma fuite des prisons de la République de Venise qu'on appelle les Plombs,* Prague 1797.

Giacomo Casanova, *Mémoires de J. Casanova de Seingalt écrits par lui-même,* Paris 1826-1838

Gaetano Cozzi, *Repubblica di Venezia e Stati Italiani,* Turin 1982.

Gaetano Cozzi (edited by), *Stato, società e Giustizia nella Repubblica Veneta (sec. XV-XVIII),* Rome 1980.

Andrea Da Mosto, *I Dogi di Venezia nella vita pubblica e privata,* Milan 1966.

Da Tiziano a El Greco. Per la storia del manierismo a Venezia, catalogue of the exhibition in the Doge's Palace, Milan 1981.

Wladimiro Dorigo,*Venezia Romanica,* Venice 2003.

Tiziano Ferro, *I capitelli del Palazzo Ducale di Venezia,* Venezia, 1995.

Robert Finlay, *Politics in Renaissance Venice,* London 1980.

Umberto Franzoi, *Il Palazzo Ducale di Venezia,* Rome 1987.

Umberto Franzoi, *Itinerari segreti nel Palazzo Ducale a Venezia,* Treviso 1983.

Umberto Franzoi, *L'Armeria di Palazzo Ducale a Venezia,* Treviso 1990.

Umberto Franzoi, *Le prigioni di Palazzo Ducale a Venezia,* Milan 1997.

Umberto Franzoi, *Storia e leggenda di Palazzo Ducale,* Venice 1982.

Deborah Howard, *Jacopo Sansovino. Architecture and Patronage in Renaissance Venice,* New Haven and London 1975.

Norbert Huse e Wolfgang Wolters, *Venedig. Die Kunst der Renaissance,* Munchen 1986.

Norbert Michael Knapton, Giovanni Scarabello, *La Repubblica di Venezia nell'età moderna,* Turin 1992.

Frederic C. Lane, *Venice. A Maritime Republic,* London 1973.

L'architettura gotica veneziana, Venice 2000.

Giulio Lorenzetti, *Venezia e il suo estuario,* Trieste 1926-2002.

Antonio Manno, *Il Poema del Tempo. I capitelli del Palazzo Ducale di Venezia Storia e iconografia,* Venice 1999.

Stefania Mason Rinaldi, *Palma il Giovane. L'opera completa,* Milan 1984.

E. Morando Di Custoza, *Libro d'armi di Venezia,* Verona 1979.

Rodolfo Pallucchini, *La pittura veneziana del Seicento,* Milan 1981.

Rodolfo Pallucchini and Paola Rossi, *Tintoretto. Le opere sacre e profane,* Milan 1984.

Filippo Pedrocco, *Veronese,* Florence 1999.

Filippo Pedrocco, *Tiziano*, Milan 2000.

Piazza San Marco, l'architettura, la storia, le funzioni, Padua 1970.

Renato Polacco (a cura di), *Storia dell'arte marciana: l'architettura*, Venice 1997.

Lionello Puppi, *Andrea Palladio*, Milan 1973.

Lionello Puppi and Loredana Olivato Puppi, *Mauro Codussi*, Milan 1977.

Claudio Rendina, *I Dogi. Storia e Segreti*. Rome 1981.

John Ruskin, *The Stones of Venice*, London 1851-1853.

Francesco Sansovino, *Lettera intorno al Palazzo Ducale e descrizione de' quadri nella Sala del Consiglio esistenti prima dell'incendio del 1577, pubblicate da Francesco Sansovino e riprodotte con illustrazioni*, Venice 1829.

Marin Sanudo il Giovane, *De origine Situ et magistratibus Urbis venetae ovvero la Città di Venezia (1493-1530)*, crit. ed. Angelo Caracciolo Aricò, Milan 1980.

Giovanni Scarabello, *Guida alla civiltà di Venezia*, Milan 1987.

Storia di Venezia, dalle origini alla caduta della Serenissima, VIII vols., Rome 1992-1998.

Manfredo Tafuri (edited by), *Renovatio Urbis. Venezia nell'età di Andrea Gritti*, Rome 1984.

Manfredo Tafuri, *Venezia e il Rinascimento. Religione, scienza, architettura*, Roma 1985.

Freddy Thinet, *Histoire de Venise*, Paris 1981.

Tiziano, catalogue of the exhibition in the Doge's Palace, Venice 1990.

Venezia e la difesa del Levante. Da Lepanto a Candia 1570-1670, catalogue of the exhibition in the Doge's Palace, Venice 1986.

Venezia l'arte nei secoli, Udine 1997.

Sarah Wilk, *The Sculpture of Tullio Lombardo. Studies in Sources and Meaning*, New York-London 1978.

Wolfgang Wolters, *Der Bilderschmuck des Dogenpalastes*, Stuttgart 1983.

Wolfgang Wolters, *La scultura veneziana gotica (1300-1460)*, Venice 1976.

Stefano Zuffi (edited by), *Capitali dell'arte: Venezia*, Milan 1999.

Photographic credits
Archivio Fotografico di Palazzo Ducale,
Venice
Archivio Musei Civici Veneziani
Archivio Mondadori Electa, Milan
courtesy Ministero per i Beni e le
Attività Culturali
Cameraphoto Arte, Venice
Francesco Turio Böhm, Venice

Graphic design of the Doge's Palace
coats-of-arms by Alessandro Paolinelli.

The axonometric drawings of the Doge's
Palace are taken from *Venezia e il Veneto*,
Dorling Kindersley Book-Arnoldo
Mondadori Editore, Milan 2003.

This volume was printed for Mondadori Electa S.p.A.
at Martellago Mondadori Printing S.p.A.,
Via Castellana 98, Martellago (Venice), in the year 2005